Introduction

William Shakespeare's 'Romeo and Juliet' is one of the most widely studied te
However, despite its popularity, very few students are able to understand the
Shakespeare's use of language was extremely complex and this makes his work both a challenge and
a huge reward for those who study it. Many teenagers will fall in love with literature through
studying Shakespeare's work, but for others it will be the final nail in the coffin that turns them away
from reading for pleasure. My aim for this eBook is to show you the beauty of Shakespeare's writing.
In this revision guide I translate the complete text into modern English. This means taking all 25,000
words and re-writing them in a way that would be easy to understand for a modern teenager or
young adult. Many people tell me that the success of my YouTube videos (over 1 million views and
counting) is due largely to the way I make complex concepts easy to understand. In this eBook I use
that skill-set to re-write the play in a way that will allow anyone to grasp what is going on. However,
I don't stop there. For every scene, I analyse key elements of language, structure and form, which
are the key assessment foci of all GCSE and A-Level English Literature courses. Perhaps most exciting
of all, the writing is interspersed with links to dozens of videos where I analyse the text. This gives
you the unique opportunity to choose between reading my work, listening to it or watching it take
place via video.

If you find this revision guide useful then please visit youtube.com/mrbruff where you will find
hundreds of videos focusing on English and English Literature. My videos have been viewed over 19
million times across 200+ nations – I'd love you to join in.

Hello

Thank you so much for purchasing this revision guide.
Everything that is covered in here is also covered in a
corresponding set of videos which I have made neat and
accessible on our terrific partner platform: **TuitionKit.**

On TuitionKit you'll be able to schedule all my revision
videos from this booklet and others to help your organise
your revision better, by breaking it down into easy to
handle bitesize chunks. You'll also find many of my other
playlists and great resources from other English teachers,
as well as super Maths and Science teachers too.

My videos are free when you sign up at
 **www.tuitionkit.com/bruffsentme** using the code
"Bruffsentme" and that code will also give you a **20%**
discount on all the other material on the site for all your
core GCSE subject revision.

To get a flavour for how TuitionKit's great features will help
you revise, go to: **www.tuitionkit.com** and sign up for your free
48 hour trial. Remember all my videos will always be free and advert-free too, so head over
to TuitionKit and get a step closer to the grades you deserve!

All the best with your studies.

Mr. Bruff

Contents

Analysis of the Play

The Origins of the Play

Although many students assume that William Shakespeare created the storyline of 'Romeo and Juliet', the truth is that it was someone else who came up with the original plot.

The Italian writer Matteo Bandello (1480-1562) is the original creator of what we now know as 'Romeo and Juliet'. He wrote the short story 'Giullette e Romeo', supposedly based on a true life story which had taken place in his home country of Italy (hence the Italian setting of Shakespeare's play). In 1562 the English poet Arthur Brooke translated the short story into a poem (along with some small plot changes which affected minor characters such as the Nurse and the Friar). Brooke died a year after publication and the now classic tale was picked up by the English novelist William Painter, who adapted it into a novel entitled 'The Palace of Pleasure' (1567). Finally, around the year 1590, William Shakespeare adapted the story for the stage, writing the play 'Romeo and Juliet'. In the 400+ years that followed, the play would go on to become one of the best known stories in the world.

Form Analysis: Prologue as Sonnet

Understanding what we are being told in the prologue is just one part of the puzzle; the next challenge is to examine the form in which it is written.

THE Sonnet Form

The sonnet is a genre of love poetry which originated in Italy in the 13th Century. The 14th Century poet Petrarch is the most recognised Italian sonneteer. Falling in love with a woman known only as 'Laura', he wrote 366 sonnets to her.

The Italian sonnet follows a strict form:

14 lines

The first 8 lines (known as the octave) present a problem

The last 6 lines (known as the sestet) present a solution to the problem

Line 9 (known as the Volta) introduces a sharp twist, or turn, which brings about the move to the resolution

ABBA ABBA rhyme scheme.

THE Shakespearean Sonnet

In the 16th Century, the sonnet made its way into English poetry. Sir Philip Sidney developed it, but it came to be known as the Shakespearean sonnet (after Shakespeare made it truly famous). This form is quite different to the Petrarchan sonnet:

It is written in iambic pentameter (lines of 10 syllables, with alternating stressed and unstressed syllables).

It is divided into 3 verses of four lines each, known as 'quatrains', and finished with a rhyming couplet which also served as the Volta.

Its rhyme scheme is also different: ABAB CDCD EFEF GG.

A close look at the prologue will reveal that it is, in fact, a Shakespearean sonnet:

Notice some key features about the prologue:

- The prologue is divided into 3 verses of four lines each, known as 'quatrains', and finished with a rhyming couplet which also served as the Volta.
- The prologue is written in iambic pentameter (lines of 10 syllables, with alternating stressed and unstressed syllables).
- The prologue contains words we would expect to see in a love poem: 'fair', 'lovers', 'love'
- The prologue has the rhyme scheme: ABAB CDCD EFEF GG

Analysis

Although Shakespeare adopted the form of a romantic love poem, he filled it with the language of hate and conflict (see the words highlighted in green) to symbolise how the play was to be a mixture of both love and conflict. Perhaps the intertwining of the two symbolises the idea that it is impossible to have the one without the other: Shakespeare seems to be suggesting that love and hate are joined together. This interpretation would tie in with many critics who see the major theme of the whole play as being a reflection of how humans are neither wholly good nor wholly bad, but a complex mix of the two. Whatever the reason, it is no coincidence that Shakespeare, only two minutes into the play, is intelligently mixing form with language to present his theme.

Character Analysis of Romeo in Act 1 Scene 1

Towards the end of Act 1 Scene 1 the audience gets to meet the first of the title characters: Romeo. As many of you will be writing about him in controlled assessments or essays, let's take a look at how Shakespeare presents our tragic hero in this scene.

Before we meet Romeo he is talked about by Montague, Lady Montague and Benvolio. All three present him as a quiet and shy character, seen when Benvolio explains that Romeo 'was ware of me and stole into the covert of the wood' (saw me and ran off into the woods to be alone). This suggests that Romeo has a reclusive personality, which is further backed up when Montague confirms that Romeo has been seen there many times 'with tears', before running home and locking himself away in 'his chamber' (his bedroom). We know from the prologue that this is the same Romeo who will take his own life, and get the sense that perhaps he is well on the way to doing so already.

In the opening of the scene, Sampson and Gregory gave us a very sexual view of love through their constant use of innuendo and double entendres such as "my naked weapon is out". Their conversation presents love as a wholly sexual thing and the audience, upon meeting Romeo, may expect his experience of love to be far more romantic.

Romeo begins by explaining that "sad hours seem long", meaning that time passes by slowly when you are unhappy in love. There is plenty of classical imagery, such as the references to "Cupid" and "Diana", and all the dramatic exaggeration and hyperbole audiences would expect from someone deeply in love, such as "Love is a smoke made with the fume of sighs". Romantic poetry in Elizabethan England often focused on how a man suffered when in love, and audiences would feel that Romeo was fitting the mould perfectly so far; up until this point Romeo seems to be a far more romantic character.

However, this romantic view of Romeo soon changes as he reveals that he is so upset because the woman he loves will not "ope her lap to saint-seducing gold". What does this mean? It means that the woman he loves will not open her legs and have sex with him, despite his best efforts. "Saint-seducing gold" could be a metaphor for Romeo's manhood, suggesting that his genitalia are so perfect that he could seduce a saint. Alternatively, it could suggest that he has gone so far as to offer the woman gold to get her to sleep with him. Either way, he has been unsuccessful.

So what do we think of Romeo now? Just like Sampson, it seems that Romeo's ideas about love and women are entirely based on sex - surely not the best first impression for our main character to make?

The Greek philosopher Aristotle, around the year 335 BC, wrote 'Poetics', a book which included theories on narrative structure. He analysed Greek tragedy as a genre and defined some of the main characteristics which he felt were essential in tragedy. The one I want to focus on here is 'hubris'.

4

Aristotle suggested that all tragedy focuses on a man of high social standing who meets his death because of his hubris - arrogance or excessive pride in some area. Tragic heroes are good people who have just one area of weakness that leads to their deaths; Romeo certainly fits this model. Could it be that Romeo's hubris is his inability to escape falling in love with every woman that he sets eyes on? This certainly fits in with the picture painted so far and the events which unfold later in the tale. Yes, it seems that Romeo is a well-liked guy who is respected by many, but he just can't keep clear of the ladies. Today he would undoubtedly end up on an episode of the 'Jeremy Kyle' show as the man who couldn't stop falling in love. This idea is backed up by the fact that the woman Romeo is currently lovesick over is not even Juliet! Surely Shakespeare starts the play with Romeo being lovesick over a different woman to suggest that Romeo is just this sort of person - he falls in love all of the time. So, Shakespeare is following the generic conventions of Greek tragedy by presenting a tragic hero whose hubris is, perhaps, his obsession with women and falling in love. Some critics have suggested that Romeo's hubris is his fearlessness about death. Either way, Romeo is tragically flawed from the start.

Contextual Analysis – Act 1 Scene 2
After the intensity and drama of Act 1 Scene 1, this following scene is relatively short and uneventful. In it we are introduced to Paris, a young man who is keen to marry Capulet's daughter Juliet. We learn that Juliet has 'not seen the change of fourteen years', meaning she is only thirteen years old. In Shakespeare's time the legal age from which a female could get married was just twelve years of age, although most women got married in their twenties just like today (in 2013 the average UK age of marriage is 28 for a woman, whereas in 1590 it was 27). However, a special exception was sometimes made for rich and noble families, who would often marry off their young children for reasons of property and family alliance. If your family had money and my family had land, our parents may want us to marry so that, through linking the families with our marriage, they have both money *and* land.

What is most interesting in this scene is how Paris is in an almost identical situation to that of Romeo in the previous scene. In Act 1 Scene 1, Benvolio tells Romeo that he should look at other beautiful women to take his mind off Rosaline, and here in Act 2 Scene 2 we see Capulet doing the same with Paris. Because Capulet thinks Juliet is too young to marry, he tells Paris to come to the party and look at other beautiful women to take his mind off Juliet. The meaning here is clear: Shakespeare is setting up the play so that Romeo and Paris are reflections of each other. Very soon we will see that both want Juliet, and therefore both are heading for the same outcome. Without giving anything away, we shall also see that the ending for both is very similar (despite the fact that the DiCaprio film doesn't show how the story ends for Paris).

The scene with the servant who cannot read is placed here for two reasons. Firstly, it is a plot device used to get Romeo to the Capulet party. Secondly, it is a moment of light humour following what has been a very heavy opening scene. Shakespeare is aiming to please everyone in the crowd: those who like action and violence, those who like romance and those who like humour.
Finally, why did Shakespeare call this character 'Paris'? In Greek mythology, Paris was the son of Priam. Invited to a great feast by Zeus, Paris was asked to look at all the beautiful goddesses and choose the most beautiful of them all: sound familiar? This classical myth reflects the current situation in 'Romeo and Juliet'. Just like the mythological Paris, Paris is invited to a feast to survey the beautiful and choose his favourite. Who will he choose? Let's read on and see!

Contextual Analysis Act 1 Scene 3
Similar to the previous scene, Act 1 Scene 3 offers a welcome dose of comedy to the play. The Nurse is a fantastic character with a bawdy, sexual sense of humour that is just as funny as that of Sampson and Gregory. Whereas the servant in Act 1 Scene 2 offered some light comedy, the Nurse

is all out slapstick in this scene. Perhaps the funniest part of this scene is where she tells a long anecdote from Juliet's childhood:

"For even the day before, she broke her brow: And then my husband—God be with his soul!
A' was a merry man—took up the child:
'Yea,' quoth he, 'dost thou fall upon thy face? Thou wilt fall backward when thou hast more wit".
After telling this long story the Nurse, proving she is a forgetful woman, repeats the whole thing once more! The juxtaposition of the uninhibited Nurse and the reserved Lady Capulet and Juliet makes the comic effect even more powerful.

However, this scene also offers an insight into the role of women in Shakespeare's time. When the baby Juliet falls over onto her face, the Nurse's husband remarks 'Thou wilt fall backward when thou comest to age'. The meaning of this line is clear: when you grow into a woman you will fall onto your back to have sex. To a modern audience this line may seem shocking - the Nurse's husband is talking to a baby girl about the sexual future that awaits her. However, an Elizabethan audience would see nothing odd here.

In Shakespeare's time, women were seen as little more than mothers and objects of male desire. Most women were denied anything beyond a basic schooling. Even when girls did go to grammar schools, many classes had 'male only' signs on the doors; girls would only be taught the most basic subjects. Upper class families (like Juliet's) would hire tutors to teach their children, but even then the prospects for an educated woman were very slim: women could not enter any profession or even vote, but instead were being prepared for domestic lives. Upper class girls were taught how to cook, sew, play instruments and do anything else which might be seen to make domestic life more attractive.

The only option for a woman was to get married and to run the household. With this in mind, we can see that the Nurse's husband was right: Juliet (and all women of the time) was fated to end up being attached to a man. Today women have no need to marry, but failure to find a husband in Shakespeare's time meant a desperate life.

Females could only survive through the men who provided for them. As children, girls would rely on their father for financial support and protection. When married, this responsibility passed onto the husband. It was almost unheard of not to marry - if a woman didn't wed there were only two other options available: become a nun or become a prostitute. This shocking contextual detail helps up to see the situation Juliet is in here.

At the time 'Romeo and Juliet was written it was illegal to marry without parental consent, meaning you needed Mum and Dad's permission to get married. Juliet's mother and father want her to marry Paris, an eligible bachelor. It is an example of dramatic irony (where the audience know more than the characters on the stage) that we already know Juliet is fated to be with Romeo, not Paris. The tension is building as we approach the party scene which will finish this first act. We know that Romeo and Juliet will be there, but so will Rosaline and Paris. How will it all unfold? Let's read on and find out!

Analysing Act 1 Scene 4
For the first time in the play we have a scene which seems unnecessary. Act 1 Scene 4 basically tells us things we already know: Romeo and his friends are heading to Capulet's party, but Romeo is not in the mood to go. Didn't we learn all of this in Act 1 Scene 2? The answer is yes!

However, the character of Mercutio is developed in this scene. His long winded speech about 'Queen Mab' may initially seem to be unimportant, but it reveals a lot about the character which will prove important further into the play.

The Queen Mab speech starts off like a child's fairytale, with images as innocent as a chariot made of 'an empty hazel-nut'. This story begins in light- hearted, fairytale-like humour. However, as the tale goes on the images get darker and darker, moving from 'lovers' brains' to soldiers 'cutting foreign throats' and finishing with 'maids' being taught how to have sex. There is a frenzied chaos to the speech, and the darkening imagery is used to symbolise the darkness and chaos that is so key to the character of Mercutio. Put simply, this speech warns us "this bloke is trouble, keep an eye on him later".

Mercutio is also used to juxtapose the views of love expressed by Romeo. Romeo's unrealistic and romantic view of love causes him to moan: 'under love's heavy burden do I sink'. Mercutio, on the other hand, offers a much more sexual view of love. In fact, every time Romeo says something, Mercutio turns it into a sexual joke. When Mercutio answers Romeo by telling him to "prick love for pricking", he is punning on the word 'prick' as a slang term for 'penis'. Once again, the two views of love: romantic or purely sexual, are contrasted in this scene. In the following scene our two title characters shall meet, and we will see which type of love wins out between the two.
It is worth noting that Shakespeare created the Queen Mab character; she did not appear in any of the earlier versions of the story of Romeo and Juliet. After her appearance in 'Romeo and Juliet', Queen Mab has gone on to appear in a wide variety of literature. It is a sign of Shakespeare's popularity that Mab makes an appearance in the 17th Century poetry of Ben Johnson. She re-appears in the 1813 poem 'Queen Mab' by Percy Shelley:

> Behold the chariot of the Fairy Queen!
> Celestial coursers paw the unyielding air;
> Their filmy pennons at her word they furl,
> And stop obedient to the reins of light;
> These the Queen of Spells drew in;
> She spread a charm around the spot,
> And, leaning graceful from the ethereal car,
> Long did she gaze, and silently,
> Upon the slumbering maid.

More famously, Queen Mab is the name of the 31st chapter of Herman Melville's 'Moby Dick' (1851) and the character even appears to Peter Pan in J.M Barrie's 'The Little White Bird' (1902):

'To Peter's bewilderment he every fairy he met fled from him of workmen who were sawing down rushed away leaving their them A milkmaid turned upside down and hid in it Soon were in an uproar Crowds were running this way and that each other stoutly who was afraid were extinguished doors barricaded from the grounds of Queen Mab's the rub a dub of drums showing royal guard had been called out of Lancers came charging Broad Walk armed with holly leaves which they jag the enemy horribly.'

This is just one example of how Shakespeare's work has influenced the literary world that followed him. Whilst we may count Queen Mab as being of little or no consequence in the play, her influence beyond it has been anything but small.

Analysing Act 1 Scene 5
Act 1 Scene 5 is the final scene of the first act. In this scene, Romeo and Juliet meet for the first time. Of course, we knew from the prologue that the two were going to fall in love, but we are still keen to see how it will happen.

Romeo experiences love at first sight the instant he sees Juliet from across the room. In that instant he forgets Rosaline, questioning "Did my heart love till now?" Although we have no doubt that Romeo has fallen in love, we are reminded of how similar his words here are to those he spoke of Rosaline in Act 1 Scene 1: "this love feel I". Shakespeare presents Romeo as a fickle character, one whose mind and opinions will change in an instant. This instantaneous love for Juliet once again backs up the hypothesis that Romeo's hubris is his inability to escape falling in love. However, there are some major differences in the way Romeo talks to and about Juliet.

In Act 1 Scene 1, we saw the source of Romeo's unhappiness was that he could not get Rosaline to have sex with him. The bawdy language our hero used left us in no doubt that he simply wanted to sleep with her. In contrast to this, let's look at the language Romeo uses when he first talks to Juliet:

ROMEO
If I profane with my unworthiest hand,
This holy shrine; the gentle fine is this;
My lips, two blushing pilgrims, ready stand
To smooth that rough touch with a tender kiss.

JULIET
Good pilgrim, you do wrong your hand too much,
Which mannerly devotion shows in this;
For saints have hands that pilgrims' hands do touch,
And palm to palm is holy palmers' kiss.

ROMEO
Have not saints lips, and holy palmers too?

JULIET
Ay, pilgrim, lips that they must use in prayer.

ROMEO
O, then, dear saint, let lips do what hands do;
They pray, grant thou, lest faith turn to despair.
JULIET
Saints do not move, though grant for prayers' sake.

ROMEO
Then move not, while my prayer's effect I take.

As you can see, both Romeo and Juliet use the language of religion to discuss their love. On top of this, Romeo is only asking to hold hands and kiss - a stark contrast to his earlier requests for sex from Rosaline. Shakespeare is changing the vocabulary of Romeo in this scene to show that his feelings for Juliet are pure and holy. But there is more than this. Take a closer look at the following (minus the names):

Notice some key features about the merged words of Romeo and Juliet:

If I profane with my unworthiest hand
This holy shrine, the gentle fine is this:
My lips, two blushing pilgrims, ready stand
To smooth that rough touch with a tender kiss.
Good pilgrim, you do wrong your hand too much,
Which mannerly devotion shows in this;
For saints have hands that pilgrims' hands do touch,
And palm to palm is holy palmers' kiss.
Have not saints lips, and holy palmers too?
Ay, pilgrim, lips that they must use in prayer.
O, then, dear saint, let lips do what hands do;
They pray, grant thou, lest faith turn to despair.
Saints do not move, though grant for prayers' sake.
Then move not, while my prayer's effect I take.

- 3 verses of four lines each, known as 'quatrains', and finished with a rhyming couplet which also serves as the Volta.
- iambic pentameter (lines of 10 syllables, with alternating stressed and unstressed syllables).
- Rhyme scheme: ABAB CDCD EFEF GG

Yes, as you can see from my annotations, this is a Shakespearean sonnet! The combined conversation between the two joins together to complete a perfect sonnet. Sonnets are a form of love poetry which have fourteen lines of iambic pentameter, with the rhyme scheme ABAB CDCD EFEF GG. Shakespeare's employment of form is here used to symbolise that the couple are perfect for each other, and complete each other. Only when united together do their words create a sonnet, symbolising how they can only find true love when joined together. The audience would feel delighted that these two, both so clearly unhappy with the way their lives were heading, have found perfect happiness.

In this scene, Romeo professes his love for Juliet in a very poetic manner. Shakespeare uses the form of a 'blason', where various parts of a woman's body are described using a range of grand metaphors. This was a very popular form of love poetry in Shakespeare's time, and Elizabethan audiences would have instantly recognised it when Romeo proclaims such lines as 'Juliet is the sun'. At first glance, it may seem that Romeo is truly in love with Juliet. However, knowing Shakespeare's wider body of work leads us to question the sincerity of this scene.

Shakespeare did not just write plays; he also wrote 154 sonnets. In Sonnet 130, he famously rejects the blazon form by writing a love poem which attacks the suggestion that women are so perfect:

SONNET 130

My mistress' eyes are nothing like the sun;
Coral is far more red than her lips' red;
If snow be white, why then her breasts are dun;
If hairs be wires, black wires grow on her head.
I have seen roses damask'd, red and white,
But no such roses see I in her cheeks;
And in some perfumes is there more delight
Than in the breath that from my mistress reeks.
I love to hear her speak, yet well I know
That music hath a far more pleasing sound;

I grant I never saw a goddess go;
My mistress, when she walks, treads on the ground:
And yet, by heaven, I think my love as rare As any she belied with false compare.

In this poem, Shakespeare is essentially saying "My woman is not surreal and perfect, like the blazon form of poetry implies. She is a normal woman who has wiry hair and bad breath, and yet I am still madly in love with her". The sonnet criticises the poetic form of the blason by suggesting it is too idealistic and unrealistic, painting women as objects of perfection that they really cannot be compared to. The sonnet concludes that real love is love which accepts the other's imperfections. With this in mind, what are we to make of Romeo's words in this scene? It is highly likely that Shakespeare gives Romeo the language of the blason in this scene to highlight how his feelings for Juliet are idealistic and unrealistic. To suggest that Juliet 'is the sun' is such an outrageously exaggerated statement, it indicates that Romeo is not in his right mind. Shakespeare is showing us the unrealistic nature of Romeo's love; just like with Rosaline, this young boy has fallen head over heels in love. In this case, with Juliet, we know that he hadn't even spoken to her before he was professing his love for her. Once again, the presentation of Romeo suggests that he is fickle. His use of the blason further backs up the analysis of his hubris: he simply cannot help himself from falling in love.

Analysing Act 2 Scene 1
The scene begins with the return of the prologue. Once again, this is a Shakespearean sonnet:

Now old desire doth in his death-bed lie,

And young affection gapes to be his heir;

That fair for which love groan'd for and would die,

With tender Juliet match'd, is now not fair.

Iambic pentameter (lines of 10 syllables, with alternating stressed and unstressed syllables).

Now Romeo is beloved and loves again,

Alike betwitched by the charm of looks,

But to his foe supposed he must complain,

And she steal love's sweet bait from fearful hooks:

Divided into 3 verses of four lines each, known as 'quatrains', and finished with a rhyming couplet which also served as the Volta.

Being held a foe, he may not have access

To breathe such vows as lovers use to swear;

And she as much in love, her means much less

To meet her new-beloved any where:

The prologue has the rhyme scheme: ABAB CDCD EFEF GG

But passion lends them power, time means, to meet

Tempering extremities with extreme sweet.

As we found at the very start of the play, here is a poem written in the form of a love poem but containing lots of language associated with death: 'Death-bed',' die' and 'groan'd' are perhaps the most obvious. Although language of death also has a double meaning associated with sex (more on that later), this prologue once again mixes form and language to foreshadow how Romeo and Juliet's love for each other will ultimately bring about their deaths.

Analysing Act 2 Scene 2
In this scene we see a return of the bawdy, sexual humour that was missing from Act 1 Scene 5. Once again, Mercutio leads the way with his remarks about Romeo sitting under a 'medlar tree'. Taking the form of a large shrub or small tree, the medlar has been farmed since Roman times. The root (no pun intended) of Mercutio's comment concerns the appearance of the fruit that comes from the medlar tree. A quick search for the tree on Google Images will show you what he had in mind with his comment, as the fruit from a medlar is thought to represent the look of a woman's genitalia.

Shakespeare was not the first to use the medlar as a symbol of sexual imagery. Chaucer, in the prologue of the Reeve's Tale (1475), refers to the medlar as a symbol of prostitution. This symbolism links not only to the genitalia-like look of the fruit, but also to the fact that the medlar fruit is rotten before it is ripe. In farming terms, it is eaten when 'bletted' (brown with rot). For Chaucer, the idea of a fruit spoiled before ripe has the sexual connotation of a woman who has had sex too early in life. Both meanings are effective in helping the audience to understand that Mercutio sees Romeo's romance as a desire for sex and nothing else.

The effect of this bawdy language is all the more powerful when juxtaposed with that of the previous scene. Up to this point, the entire play has been filled with sexual banter and innuendo. From Sampson and Gregory at the start, to Romeo's anger at Rosaline's closed 'lap', to the Nurse's swearing by her childhood virginity, the language has been highly sexual. However in Act 1 Scene 5, as we saw previously, the language was religious and pure. By following that scene with this – another highly sexualised scene, Shakespeare is using structure to show just how pure and perfect the love of Romeo and Juliet is.

Analysing Act 2 Scene 3
Shakespeare uses the literary device of foreshadowing to hint at future events which are yet to come in the play. The scene begins with Friar Laurence carrying a basketful of plants. He explains that these plants have a multitude of uses: some are medicinal and others, 'being tasted, slay all senses within the heart.' It is no co-incidence that the Friar talks of poisonous plants that cause death when tasted. If you don't know the ending of the play then please skip the rest of this paragraph. For those who do, this talk of poison foreshadows how Romeo will take his life in Act 5 Scene 3. In fact, the play is packed full of foreshadowing, to the point that it is often so blatant and obvious it comes across as laughable. There are two major purposes of this foreshadowing. On the one hand, it makes later events easier to understand for those in the audience who struggle to follow the plot. Secondly, and perhaps most importantly, it ties into the theme of fate.
Those who believe in fate believe that the events of their lives are pre- determined and set – there is nothing that can be done to avoid them. We know from the prologue that 'Romeo and Juliet' is a play which revolves around the theme of 'star-cross'd lovers'. The meaning of the term 'star-cross'd' can be translated as 'fated'. So, if the events in the play are fated to take place, the foreshadowing of poison as a cause of death seen is this scene is a small hint that everything which is to come is already predetermined. Romeo's suicide by poisoning is foreshadowed here, and is a reminder that fate controls everything in the play.

When Romeo visits the Friar and tells him how he has not slept all night, the Friar wrongly guesses: 'Was thou with Rosaline?' It is clear from this quotation that the Friar knows Romeo well and also knows of his previous love for Rosaline. He even challenges Romeo, asking if Rosaline is 'so soon forsaken'. The audience sees that the Friar seems to have the true measure of Romeo as a fickle youth, which makes it doubly confusing when the Friar agrees to marry Romeo and Juliet in Act 2 Scene 6. A detailed character analysis of the Friar shall be completed later in this guide.

When Romeo explains to the Friar that he was only sad over Rosaline because she did not return his love, the Friar responds with 'She knew well, thy love did read by rote and could not spell'. What he is saying here is that Rosaline knew that Romeo's love was not real – he was just 'trying it on'. What does this tell us about Romeo? Was he deliberately aiming to mislead Rosaline into believing he loved her so that he could have sex with her? The alternative interpretation is that Rosaline knew Romeo's feelings were not genuine, even though Romeo himself thought they were. Either presentation doesn't exactly paint Romeo in strong colours.

Analysing Act 2 Scene 4

As in the previous scene, there is a strong sense of foreshadowing in Act 2 Scene 4. Mercutio tells Benvolio: 'Alas poor Romeo! he is already dead'. He is talking in jest about Romeo being dead in love, but of course what he says will soon come true. Once again this heavy reliance on foreshadowing backs up the major theme of fate – that the events in the play are pre-determined and set.

Perhaps sensing that the plot was becoming too serious, Shakespeare introduces humour through the Nurse's use of malapropisms. A malapropism is the misuse of a word for humorous effect. The word which is used sounds similar to the correct word but has a very different meaning. When the Nurse tells Romeo 'I'll tell her that you do protest; which, as I take it, is a gentlemanlike offer', she makes an error in her use of the word 'protest'. What she means to say is 'I will tell her that you propose, which is gentlemanlike offer'. As you can see, the undesired meaning is the complete opposite of what was meant: a funny moment when you add it together with the other examples we see from the nurse in this scene.

Time plays a key role in Act 2 Scene 4. Romeo tells the Nurse that Juliet should meet him at the Church 'this afternoon' to be married. Having met the previous evening, Romeo and Juliet will be married within 24 hours of meeting. From their initial meeting to their marriage they will speak only a thousand or so words each. The audience is surely left wondering how real this love can be. In the previous scene Friar Laurence scolded Romeo's professions of love for Rosaline by telling him 'Thy love did read by rote and could not spell.' It seems Rosaline knew that Romeo's love for her was not real, but thirteen year old.

Juliet is bewitched by him. Is this a true example of love at first sight, or is our tragic hero Romeo once again exhibiting his hubris by falling in love once more? Of course, there are many who believe that Romeo is truly in love. It is possible that Romeo, now reformed from his previous wicked ways, is devoted to Juliet in all sincerity. This has certainly been the traditional interpretation of the character over the years. However, if you are studying this text for an assessment of some kind, it is always useful to offer alternative interpretations. This means that you take a quotation and offer more than one possible meaning. At the end of the day, none of us knows exactly what Shakespeare meant through his presentation of Romeo, but an open mind to a variety of interpretations will help you improve your grade.

Analysing Act 2 Scene 5

At first glance it is possible to see this scene as nothing more than a comic interlude in the plot. It is true that the conversation between Juliet and her Nurse is highly amusing, with the Nurse essentially winding Juliet up by delaying the news of Romeo's wedding proposal. However, there is more to it than that.

Following the romance which has blossomed between Romeo and Juliet at shocking speed, this scene deliberately slows things down to add tension and suspense before building up to the wedding scene. Dramatic structure is explored elsewhere in this book, but it is true to say that Shakespeare was a master of pace and structure; he knew that it would be an overload of emotion to have fighting, romance, love and death in every scene. Because of this, he occasionally intersperses the action with scenes that slow down the pace and give the audience time to calm down (and to take stock of everything that has just happened). If you are at the theatre and need a toilet break, this might be the time to take it!

What is striking in this short scene is the immaturity of Juliet, who becomes an impatient child in this interchange. She is rude and demanding of the Nurse: 'Is they news good, or bad? Answer to that'. This is a direct contrast to the Juliet who so eloquently and romantically confessed her love to Romeo. Perhaps Shakespeare is reminding the audience that Juliet is only thirteen years old – just a child. If she is so emotional that she has these kinds of childish outbursts at the woman who has raised her, can we really trust her feelings of the love that she has for Romeo? It is also a sign that the relationship between Juliet and her nurse continues to grow apart. Juliet, who doted on her nurse at the start of the play, is becoming a woman and moving beyond such childish things as needing what is essentially a full time babysitter. She is approaching that period of her life to which the Nurse's husband so crudely alluded; she is coming to a time in her life when she will 'fall backward' for her lover. As a result, she is starting to distance herself from the people she associates with childhood. Juliet and the Nurse will continue to grow apart throughout the play; it is a topic I shall revisit later.

Analysing Act 2 Scene 6

Act 2 Scene 6 begins with yet more foreshadowing, as Friar Laurence hopes that the heavens will 'smile' upon the marriage of Romeo and Juliet. He worries that they 'chide us not', foreshadowing the tragic events that will follow in just the next scene. Romeo takes it one step further with the challenge 'love- devouring death do what he dare' (death can do what it likes). Finally, the Friar foreshadows Juliet's death when he comments that 'so light a foot will ne'er wear out the everlasting flint'. His words suggest that Juliet is too dainty to survive the difficult road of life. Shakespeare's use of structure means that this is the perfect place to foreshadow the doom that will soon fall on our title characters.

Aristotle (see Part 5) came up with some of the earliest ideas about dramatic structure in dramatic tragedy. He felt that drama fell into three pieces. In the 19th Century, building on the work of Aristotle, the German novelist Gustav Freytag proposed that all five act plays follow the same format:

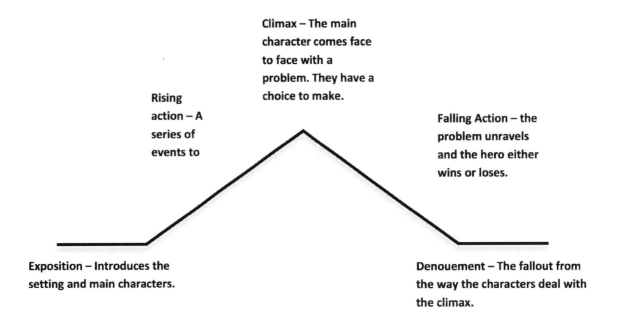

Climax – The main character comes face to face with a problem. They have a choice to make.

Rising action – A series of events to

Falling Action – the problem unravels and the hero either wins or loses.

Exposition – Introduces the setting and main characters.

Denouement – The fallout from the way the characters deal with the climax.

Freytag's theory was that all plays dedicated one act to each of the above. If we apply this to what we have already seen in 'Romeo and Juliet' the analysis would be as follows:

Act 1: Exposition – The audience discover that the Montague and Capulet families are enemies. They fight.
Act 2: Rising Action – Romeo and Juliet fall in love and get married.
Act 3: Climax – about to happen!

With this in mind, we know that the climax of the play is coming in the very next scene. Tension is high, and Shakespeare uses the literary device of foreshadowing prior to this major act to increase the tension even further.

Analysing Act 3 Scene 1

Following his secret marriage to Juliet in the previous scene, Romeo is instantly forced to face the reality of the fact that he has married a Capulet. In Act 3 Scene 1, Tybalt is hunting for Romeo; he wants to punish him for sneaking into the Capulet family party. Now that he has married into the Capulet family, Romeo wants to avoid a fight. He uses language that seems more fitting for his previous conversations with Juliet, telling Tybalt that he does 'love thee better than thou canst devise'. This line is very similar to his previous comments about Juliet in Act 2 Scene 2, where Romeo proclaims 'It is my love! O, that she knew she were.' In both examples, Romeo loves someone who doesn't know that they are loved. This mirroring of language is used to show what a dramatic change Romeo has undertaken. His bawdy banter has gone, his anger towards the Capulets has gone; now all he feels is love.

Blank verse, prose and rhyming verse are used for effect in this scene. Before I analyse them, let me give you a simple definition of each one:

Blank verse: Does not rhyme, but follows a regular pattern of rhythm. Lines of blank verse contain ten syllables per line.

Prose: We may refer to this as 'ordinary written language'. There is no rhyme scheme or metrical structure.

Rhyming verse: Lines which rhyme (often rhyming couplets where the final word of a pair of lines rhymes).

In Act 3 Scene 1, Shakespeare uses a mixture of blank verse, prose and rhyming verse to convey meaning. Firstly, most characters speak in blank verse, as seen when the scene opens with Benvolio's plea to Mercutio:

> *I pray thee, good Mercutio, let's retire:*
> *The day is hot, the Capulets abroad,*
> *And, if we meet, we shall not scape a brawl;*
> *For now, these hot days, is the mad blood stirring.*

These lines are ordered and tightly controlled – a reflection of the character of Benvolio who is the same.

The character of Mercutio, on the other hand, always speaks in prose:

> *Thou art like one of those fellows that when he*
> *enters the confines of a tavern claps me his sword*
> *upon the table and says 'God send me no need of*
> *thee!' and by the operation of the second cup draws*
> *it on the drawer, when indeed there is no need.*

As you can see from this example, Mercutio's lines are not only different to everyone else's, they are uncontrolled and follow no rules or regulations. Shakespeare is cleverly using prose for Mercutio to mirror his character; just like blank verse, he is uncontrolled and follows no rules or regulations. He is unpredictable unlike any other character: just like prose.

Finally, Montague, Prince and Lady Capulet speak in rhyming verse in this scene:

LADY CAPULET

> *He is a kinsman to the Montague;*
> *Affection makes him false; he speaks not true:*
> *Some twenty of them fought in this black strife, And all those twenty could but kill one life.*
> *I beg for justice, which thou, prince, must give; Romeo slew Tybalt, Romeo must not live.*

PRINCE

> *Romeo slew him, he slew Mercutio;*
> *Who now the price of his dear blood doth owe?*

MONTAGUE

> *Not Romeo, prince, he was Mercutio's friend;*
> *His fault concludes but what the law should end,*

This use of rhyming verse shows how these characters are separate from the others. Also, Shakespeare often uses rhyming verse when his characters are delivering advice or pointing out a moral; this is exactly what is happening in this scene.

As you can see, Shakespeare's use of blank verse, prose and rhyming verse is used to symbolise different aspects of each character's personality. Look out for its use in other scenes.

This is a very tense scene, made more powerful by the manner in which Shakespeare structures it. At first Romeo tries to stop the fighting between Mercutio and Tybalt, asking his kinsman to 'put thy rapier up'. In terms of dramatic tension, the audience would feel a sense of disappointment at this – many would want to shout out, "Go on, Romeo, kill him!" This makes the latter part of the scene even more satisfying. Having spent the earlier moments trying to unsuccessfully split up the fight between Mercutio and Tybalt, Romeo then contradicts himself and asks Tybalt to fight. As an audience we understand that Romeo is distraught at Mercutio's death; clearly 'fire-eyed fury' has taken over him.

As Mercutio is dying, he delivers one of the most famous lines from the play, calling for 'a plague on both your houses'. Again, this is an example of Shakespeare foreshadowing the end of the play where indeed a disaster will come upon both the Capulets and Montagues.

Analysing Act 3 Scene 2
The next two scenes show the different reactions to Romeo's banishment. In this scene, Juliet receives the news of Tybalt's death and Romeo's exile. For a few lines she gives an angry outburst, but this changes very quickly. Within moments, Juliet is rationally calculating the cause of the situation: 'But, wherefore, villain, didst thou kill my cousin? That villain cousin would have kill'd my husband'. She wonders why Romeo killed Tybalt and correctly guesses that it is because Tybalt was trying to kill him. As we shall see in the next scene, Juliet's mature response is very different to that of Romeo. We start to see Juliet as a girl wise beyond her years, and are perhaps swayed towards the idea that she is wise enough to make her own choices in love. Certainly she has grown more mature since her argument with the Nurse.

Light and dark play a key part in this scene. Juliet is desperate for night to arrive, telling the sun to 'gallop apace'. Darkness has offered sanctuary to the couple throughout the play – they met at night and first had sex at night. Tragically, both will die at night too. With so much of Romeo and Juliet's relationship taking place at night, Shakespeare is highlighting how the lovers are set apart from the rest of world. Living when the rest of the world sleeps, they have an almost mystical quality. Juliet's relationship with the Nurse continues to show signs of wear in this scene. The two had an incredibly close relationship in Act 1 Scene 3, where Juliet seemed to love the Nurse more than her own mother. However, here we find that the Nurse unable to understand why Juliet is siding with Romeo after Tybalt's death. She proclaims 'Will you speak well of him that kill'd your cousin?' This relationship will, by the end of the play, fall apart completely. Perhaps this symbolises how Juliet is maturing and growing into a woman; as her relationship with Romeo develops she no longer seems to need a Nurse. The transition Juliet is making from child to adult is reflected in her gradual separation from the Nurse who raised her through her childhood.

Analysing Act 3 Scene 3
In the previous scene we saw Juliet's mature and responsible reaction to the news of Romeo's banishment. In this scene we see Romeo's completely opposite response.

Romeo's reaction to the news of his banishment is dramatic and over the top. He throws himself on the floor and refuses to move, crying out, 'Be merciful, say death'. It is worth taking a moment to think rationally about the punishment which has been announced. In Act 1 Scene 1, the Prince promised that anyone who disturbed the peace of the streets again would be put to death. Romeo, therefore, is expecting to hear that his punishment is death. If this punishment was announced Romeo would not hand himself in; he would flee. He would run away to another city and hide out there. We know this from the fact that he ran away from the murder scene in the first place – he isn't going to accept the death penalty. Now let's look at the actual punishment: banishment. This is a word we don't use much these days, but it basically means that Romeo is not allowed to live in the city of Verona anymore. He is free to live in a different city, but cannot step foot in Verona. Now let's think about this – if he had been sentenced to death, Romeo would have run away and been in hiding his whole life. Now he is sentenced to banishment he can run away and start a new life with Juliet in a new city. It is clear from this that his reaction is ridiculous.

Secondly, we expect Juliet to be upset, as the news of Tybalt's death and Romeo's part in it is not something she already knew about. However, Romeo has no right to be so upset –he chose to kill Tybalt, knowing full well the Prince's punishment and the issues it would cause with Juliet. With these two points in mind, Romeo has no reason to be so dramatic here. As the Friar says, news of banishment is 'a gentler judgement' than that which was expected. Romeo refuses to accept this, claiming that 'There is no world without Verona walls'. Our narrow minded hero cannot think that there is possibly a world outside of his city.

The Nurse interrupts the scene, explaining that Juliet wants to see him. Hearing this, temperamental Romeo suddenly feels much better, proclaiming, 'How well my comfort is revived by this'. At this point the audience is surely losing patience with Romeo – following his feelings is like taking a ride on an emotional rollercoaster. Even in this scene he starts distraught and finishes elated.
Once again Shakespeare employs the literary device of foreshadowing in this scene. When Romeo announces, 'I may sack the hateful mansion', he is threatening to commit suicide. The Friar tells him to 'Hold thy desperate hand', but in Act 5 Scene 3 he will arrive at a similar scene too late to intervene.

Analysing Act 3 Scene 4
Act 3 Scene 4 is a scene where we see a different side to Lord Capulet. In Act 1 Scene 2 he told Paris to 'woo' Juliet and pursue her. Capulet made it clear that Juliet's agreement was an essential part of the marriage arrangement. Here in Act 3 Scene 2, some twenty four hours later, he seems to have changed his mind. He tells Paris that Juliet 'will be ruled in all respects by me' and sets the wedding date. This is an example of dramatic irony, where the audience know more than the characters on stage. Sitting in the audience, we know that Juliet is already secretly married to Romeo. Shakespeare uses dramatic irony to increase the tension in this scene – what will happen when the powerful and demanding Lord Capulet makes a demand of his daughter that she is unable to agree to? The stakes are raised even higher because Capulet has now made the promise to Paris and will surely not want to back down and lose face in front of this noble man.

Capulet is keen for his daughter to marry as soon as possible, setting the date for 'Wednesday next' before realising that it is already Monday. His eagerness contrasts the Friar's previous advice to Romeo in Act 2 Scene 3, who is told that 'they stumble that run fast'. It's a shame the Friar isn't on hand to offer the same advice to Capulet. Some people think that one of the play's major themes is the battle between young and old, with Romeo and Juliet essentially rebelling against adult advice throughout. However, this moment shows that it's not as simple as that – even respected adults disagree in their advice. Of course, neither the Friar nor Capulet end up getting what they want: Romeo marries right away and Juliet does not marry Paris. Once again this ties into the theme of fate. Despite their best efforts, the Friar and Capulet are unable to stop the course Romeo and Juliet are on. It is pre-determined that these 'star- cross'd lovers' will meet, fall in love and very shortly end their own lives.

Capulet's sudden change in mood gives us a hint at how the 'ancient grudge' between the Montagues and Capulets may have stayed alive for so long. He is rash, hot-headed and contradictory: not an easy person to keep the peace with.

Being such a hot-headed and contradictory character, the audience would be full of tension about the chaos they know is coming. We know that Juliet is not going to do as her father plans; we know this from the fact that Paris isn't even mentioned in the prologue. From the outset we know this play is about Romeo and Juliet, but with such a hot-headed character as Capulet being Juliet's father, it is clear that conflict is on its way.

As discussed earlier in the book, Juliet is seen as the possession of her father – he has no doubt that she will do as she is told. This seems shocking to most audiences today, but in Elizabethan times it would not have had such a big impact. The interesting point here is how audiences respond differently over time. In most exam specifications you are credited for giving 'alternative interpretations' and an easy way to do that here is to simply write about how a modern audience's reaction would differ to that of an Elizabethan audience.

Analysing Act 3 Scene 5
This scene is all about contrast. To begin, Juliet and Romeo have had their first night together in bed. Shakespeare uses over exaggerated language to show just how in love they are. Juliet argues that the sun is not the sun but is, in fact 'some meteor that the sun exhales, to be to thee this night a torch-bearer'. She argues that the sun has fired out a meteor, which will be a light to guide Romeo on his way home to Mantua. This kind of passionate exaggeration is one of the conventions of courtly love. Courtly love is a historical conception which centres on two members of the nobility who secretly love each other. In literature, tales of courtly love always include examples of passionate exaggeration and imagery related to nature. As we can see in this quotation, Juliet includes both in her comments to Romeo. Shakespeare is here using the well-known conventions of courtly love to highlight just how much the couple love each other.

The loving relationship with Romeo is juxtaposed with the relationship Juliet has with Lord Capulet. Shakespeare uses structure, putting both relationships next to each other in one scene, to heighten the difference between the two.

The relationship between Juliet and her father is one where he is possessive and controlling. In Act 3 Scene 5 Juliet refuses to do as her father says and marry Paris. He then insults her by calling her 'baggage'. This suggests that, just like a bag, she is a burden to him - a weight that weighs him down, and an accessory. It suggests that she is his possession to do with as he pleases. Just like a bag, she is unimportant to him. Juliet would have been heartbroken to be called this, but an Elizabethan audience would have sided with her father. This is because, in the 1500s, arranged marriages were normal for middle class families. It was very acceptable for your parents to choose who you marry and the audience would have agreed that Juliet should follow her father's instruction. A modern audience would be outraged, as women's rights have moved on and a modern viewer would believe that Juliet should be able to do as she pleases. Once again, by writing about the audience response over the years you are able to offer valid alternative interpretations.

Analysing Act 4 Scene 1
Friar Laurence is an interesting character to analyse. Throughout the play he is the trusted adviser of both Romeo and Juliet. The Friar is seen as a wise and intelligent character, despite the fact that the advice he gives and the actions he takes are often bizarre and unwise. Already in the play he has secretly married Romeo to Juliet, even though he knows full well how Romeo has been madly in love before with Rosaline. The Friar even gives advice about not taking things too quickly, warning that

'they stumble that run fast'. Quite why the Friar gives this advice and then ignores it is difficult to see.

In this scene, the Friar advises Juliet to 'undertake a thing like death' by swallowing a potion that will make her appear dead. His plan is to take her seemingly dead body to the family tomb, where Romeo will meet her and the two elope. This is a very strange plan – why can't Juliet just run away to Mantua and be with Romeo? When she elopes she will be forfeiting all claim to her father's riches, so why doesn't she just refuse to marry Paris and take the same punishment which was threatened by her father (that he would disown her from his wealth).

The most significant aspect of the Friar's character is how both Romeo and Juliet blindly follow him and do what he says. In this scene Juliet tells him 'bid me leap...and I will do it'. It is clear that the Friar has the unquestioning following of these youngsters, and as such can decide whatever he wants for them. When Juliet thinks of killing herself, she tells the Friar that he only needs to 'call my resolution wise' and give it his blessing and she will do it.

So why do these characters have blind faith in Friar Laurence? Perhaps it is because he is a Friar – a Catholic priest. Is Shakespeare here using the rash and bizarre actions of the Friar to criticise those in society who blindly follow the leadership of the Church? Is he calling out for people to judge wisely the actions they are being advised to take, and not follow blindly the leading of Catholicism? In Elizabethan England there was tension between Catholics and Protestants, and perhaps Shakespeare is here criticising Catholicism. There is no hard evidence to explain Shakespeare's own religious beliefs, but this is one interpretation of the character of Friar Laurence. Put yourself in Romeo and Juliet's shoes: would you follow the Friar's advice?

Analysing Act 4 Scene 2
In Act 4 Scene 2 we find Capulet busy in preparation for the wedding of Paris and Juliet. Once again, the audience knows this wedding will not take place; this use of dramatic irony indicates that Capulet is not as wise and powerful as he seems to think he is.

Once again time plays a key role in the drama unfolding before us. Capulet, ever the rash and impetuous man that he is, decides to bring the wedding forward twenty four hours. He is so delighted at Juliet's fake apology that he wants to 'have this knot knit up to-morrow morning'. The audience knows that this means there is one day less to get the message to Romeo about the fake death, and early signs of tension begin to mount as we see that things might not go to plan.

The relationship between Lord and Lady Capulet is worth exploring in this scene. When Lord Capulet announces that the wedding day will be brought forward, his wife is not in agreement, responding "No, not till Thursday; there is time enough". Capulet does not even respond to her, simply ignoring her and telling the Nurse, 'Go with her: we'll to church tomorrow'. This interchange gives the audience a glimpse of the type of marriage Juliet is so keen to avoid. Women in Elizabethan England were the property of their husbands and had no rights of their own. Lady Capulet (and all wives) had no power over her own life and no right to make decisions. Juliet, on the other hand, has taken control of her own life and is making decisions. The irony is that her decisions do not end well. Is Shakespeare saying that women should not rebel against the role they are given as submissive wives? When Juliet does so, it does not end well for her. Or is he perhaps arguing that society needs to change: gender roles, arranged marriage and the role of parents need to change in order for people to live a truly happy life?

Analysing Act 4 Scene 3

Act 4 Scene 3 sees Juliet fake her death. This scene also signifies the end of her relationship with her nurse and mother.

It is possible to interpret this scene as a metaphor for growing up. On maturing from a girl to a woman, Juliet's childhood dies and she no longer needs the things of her youth: a nurse and mother. We see this when Lady Capulet asks Juliet if she needs her help, to which her daughter replies, 'No, madam'. This is very cold behaviour from Juliet, who knows that this is the last time she will see her mother. Similarly, there is no fond farewell to the Nurse. Juliet simply tells her mother to 'let the Nurse this night sit up with you'. Juliet has transformed throughout this play, from a young girl who doted on and depended on her nurse, to a young woman who no longer needs nurse or woman. Her 'death' in this scene puts an end to childhood. If everything went as planned, Juliet's new life the next day would be that of a married woman who had no contact with or dependence upon her parents.

This new found declaration of independence is also found later in the scene. Having told her mother and nurse to leave, she begins to worry about the situation she is in and panics about the 'terror of the' tomb to which she is heading. For a moment she loses her nerve and calls the Nurse back, but soon realises that she needs to 'act alone'. Juliet has outgrown the Nurse and her mother. She has been betrayed by them in Act 3 Scene 5 (with the Nurse advising a second marriage to Paris and her mother refusing to comfort her after her father's tirade) and has realised that they can help her no further. This ties in very neatly with the reality of growing up and becoming an adult; there comes a time when you realise that your parents are not as perfect as you thought them to be. Juliet has reached that moment here and is determined to start her new life independent of both parents and nurse.

Analysing Act 4 Scene 4

Knowing that Juliet has taken the potion, the audience is keen to see what happens to her. However, Shakespeare gives us a scene here which will not answer any of our questions. In Act 4 Scene 4, Capulet and Lady Capulet are organising the wedding. It is a brief scene which includes the final comic moments of the play before the tragic final Act.

Shakespeare uses irony in the final line of the scene when Capulet orders, 'Make haste; the bridegroom he is come already'. Capulet is referring to Paris, but little does he know that Juliet is already 'dead' upstairs. In the next scene he will explain that 'Death is my son-in-law'. In this sense, the bridegroom truly has already arrived.

Analysing Act 4 Scene 5

This final scene in Act 4 focuses on the discovery of Juliet's death. It is interesting to see how the different characters react to this death.

Firstly, Lady Capulet says that Juliet was her 'one thing to rejoice and solace in'. She follows this up by telling Juliet to wake up or 'I will die with thee'. This is the first time in the entire play that Lady Capulet has seemed to care for Juliet. Up until this point Lady Capulet has been distant with her daughter. This is perhaps most notable in the Act 1 Scene 3 where she asks the nurse to 'give leave awhile' so that she can speak to Juliet in private. Right away Lady Capulet realises that this is too intimate and calls the Nurse 'back again'. In Act 3 Scene 5, when Juliet appeals to her for help in delaying the wedding to Paris, her mother coldly tells her, 'Talk not to me...I have done with thee'. It is therefore quite a shock to see Lady Capulet seem to be so caring. Unfortunately, her comments come too late at this point. This moment is a reminder not to take our loved ones for granted.

Lord Capulet's reaction seems gruesome and horrifying. He relates the death of Juliet to sexual imagery, describing how she is 'deflowered' by death. This mirrors Juliet's own words in Act 3 Scene 2 where she offers 'death, not Romeo, take my maidenhead.' To a modern audience, this linking of sex and death seems tasteless, but an Elizabethan audience would react in a different manner.

In Elizabethan England, "le petit mort" or 'a little death' was a euphemism for an orgasm. Shakespeare (and other writers) often punned on the word 'die' to mean 'to orgasm'. In fact, Juliet herself is referring to this in when she says, 'Give me my Romeo, and when I shall die'. And so, even though it seems odd today, Capulet's linking of death to sex is not as bizarre as it seems. If you study other Shakespeare plays, look carefully for this hidden euphemism; Shakespeare uses it a lot. It can be seen across many of his plays, such as the moment in 'Much Ado About Nothing' when Benedick tells Beatrice he will ' live in thy heart, die in thy lap'.

Analysing Act 5 Scene 1
In Act 1 Scene 4, Romeo was told that 'dreamers often lie', a comment which is proven to be true in this scene. Whilst we might expect Romeo to be depressed in this scene, we actually find him in a happy mood following the 'joyful news' of his dream. When Balthasar turns up, his dream is quickly shattered as he hears of Juliet's death.

Romeo reacts with anger at fate, shouting, 'I defy you stars'. Once again, the language of the prologue is referenced, and we can now see just how 'star- cross'd' these lovers seem to be. The word 'defy' is worth closer study. Romeo is not complaining to fate but is outright challenging it. Considering how large a role fate has played up until this point, this seems a stupid thing to do. Those who feel that Romeo is an immature and temperamental character can easily use this moment to back up this interpretation. It's the equivalent of approaching the toughest kid in school, spitting in his face and shouting, "Come and have a go if you think you're hard enough!"

Dramatic irony runs throughout this scene, as the audience is well aware that Juliet is not actually dead. The Friar knows this, Juliet knows this, the audience knows this, but Romeo and Balthasar do not. Having watched the play quite a few times, I can testify to the fact that audiences at this point seem to temporarily forget the prologue's news that both would end up dead. Audiences hope that somehow everything will work out OK. It is a sign of Shakespeare's powerful skill that we get so involved in the plot – we desperately want these two to be OK, but deep down we know we are kidding ourselves.

Romeo's next action tells us something key about his character. He explains that there is an apothecary (like a pharmacist) whom he had previously spotted. Because the apothecary is poor and worn down by 'sharp misery', he has guessed that he would sell him an illegal poison if he needed one. What is important here is the fact that Romeo has previously calculated that 'if a man did need a poison...here lives a caitiff wretch would sell it him.' This is very bizarre behaviour. Let's put this into perspective: what sane and rational person goes through life looking for the nearest and most convenient method of suicide, just in case they may wish to kill themselves? Here Shakespeare once again shows us how fickle Romeo is – as a tragic hero he is over emotional and irrational. This irrationality led him to fall in love with Rosaline, to be distraught when she didn't love him back, to fall in love with Juliet, to be distraught at the news of banishment and now to desire his own death. Romeo is too rash and ultimately brings about his own downfall through his actions.

Analysing Act 5 Scene 2
There is really only one thing to write about this short scene. Once again, fate controls the events of the play. Despite the Friar's greatest efforts to get a message to Romeo we learn that Friar John was

'stay'd' and the message did not get delivered. Friar Laurence, spotting what is likely to happen next, calls for 'an iron crow' (a metal crow bar) and heads off for Juliet's tomb.

As we saw after Juliet's poison scene, Shakespeare adds tension to his play by placing small 'filler' scenes in the way when the audience simply want to hurry ahead and find out what is going to happen to Romeo and Juliet. This is one way that Shakespeare uses structure to create tension.

Analysing Act 5 Scene 3
Once again the setting of night is used to bring Romeo and Juliet together. They professed their love at night, consummated their marriage at night and will now die at night. This use of setting has been employed by Shakespeare throughout the play to symbolise how the two lovers are set apart from the rest of the world. This could be to highlight how their love is 'out of this world', but there is also another interpretation to be made. Night time is the time of dreams, and the fact that Romeo and Juliet's relationship takes place largely at night could symbolise how their love is a dream – a fantasy. As Mercutio told us in Act 1 Scene 4 'dreamers often lie'. Could the setting of night here be used to show that Romeo and Juliet, just as in a dream, were lying to themselves to ever imagine their love could survive?

Paris comes out of the shadows and challenges Romeo to fight. Just as he tried at first to resist fighting Tybalt, Romeo tries to avoid conflict with Paris. He warns Paris to 'fly hence', but Paris persists and is killed. With Tybalt and now with Paris, it seems that these characters were fated to die and Romeo was unable to avoid being involved. Again, this reflects the theme of fate: Romeo tried to avoid the conflict with both, but was unable to do so.

The manner in which Romeo and Juliet die forms the final piece of the puzzle when analysing their characters. Romeo takes the easy option, having asked the pharmacist specifically for drugs which are 'quick'. His desire is an instantaneous and pain free death and he is given it, dying with the words 'thy drugs are quick'.

Juliet, on the other hand, suffers a much more gruesome death. Picking up Romeo's 'happy dagger' she stabs herself. Even when offered escape by the Friar, she rejects the offer. In many cultures (Roman and Japanese for two) death by stabbing was seen as an honourable and brave way to die. Like the Seppuku of the Japanese Samurai, Juliet's suicide through stabbing is far more impressive than Romeo's quick exit. This is just another example of Juliet proving herself to be more mature than Romeo. It echoes the characters' juxtaposed reactions to the news of Romeo's banishment, where Juliet calculated wisely and Romeo acted like a spoilt child.
Now we have reached the end of the tale, let's revisit Freytag's Pyramid:

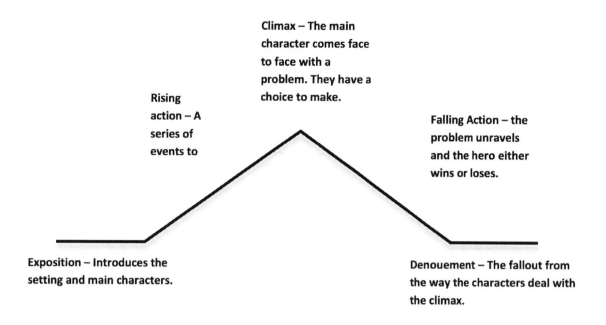

Climax – The main character comes face to face with a problem. They have a choice to make.

Rising action – A series of events to

Falling Action – the problem unravels and the hero either wins or loses.

Exposition – Introduces the setting and main characters.

Denouement – The fallout from the way the characters deal with the climax.

If we apply this to 'Romeo and Juliet' the analysis would be as follows:

Act 1: Exposition – The audience discovers that the Montague and Capulet families are enemies. They fight.
Act 2: Rising Action – Romeo and Juliet fall in love and get married.
Act 3: Climax – Tybalt kills Mercutio, Romeo kills Tybalt, Romeo is banished.
Act 4: Falling Action - Being forced to marry Paris, Juliet decides to kill herself.
Act 5: Denouement – Romeo kills Paris, Romeo kills himself, Juliet kills herself and the families are united.

The play ends in irony; the death of Romeo and Juliet brings the Capulet and Montague family together. This means that the very same problem that prevented them from marrying openly (their families being at war) is solved with their deaths. If they were somehow able to re-animate back to life, they would be able to marry and live happily ever after!

Act 1 Prologue

ORIGINAL TEXT:	MODERN TRANSLATION:
The Prologue	(An introductory speech)
Two households, both alike in dignity,	Two families, both equally good & honourable,
In fair Verona, where we lay our scene,	In the Italian city of Verona, where the play takes place,
From ancient grudge break to new mutiny,	An old resentment will once again start up,
Where civil blood makes civil hands unclean.	Where the public will end up joining in the fight.
From forth the fatal loins of these two foes	From the children of these two enemy families
A pair of star-cross'd lovers take their life;	Two fated lovers will kill themselves;
Whose misadventured piteous overthrows	Following the events which keep them apart
Do with their death bury their parents' strife.	The lovers' deaths bring the families together.
The fearful passage of their death-mark'd love,	The events which lead to the lovers' suicide,
And the continuance of their parents' rage,	And the war between the families,
Which, but their children's end, nought could remove,	Which only stopped when the lovers died,
Is now the two hours' traffic of our stage;	Is what this two hour play is all about;
The which if you with patient ears attend,	If you listen carefully,
What here shall miss, our toil shall strive to mend.	Anything you've missed from this introduction will be explained to you.

Act 1 Scene 1

ORIGINAL TEXT	MODERN TRANSLATION
SCENE I. Verona. A public place.	**Scene 1. A public area in the Italian city of Verona.**
Enter SAMPSON and GREGORY, of the house of Capulet, armed with swords and bucklers	*SAMPSON and GREGORY, two of the Capulet men, enter armed with weapons.*
SAMPSON Gregory, o' my word, we'll not carry coals.	**SAMPSON** Gregory, we will not put up with insults.
GREGORY No, for then we should be colliers.	**GREGORY** No, for that would make us worthless (like coal-miners).
SAMPSON I mean, an we be in choler, we'll draw.	**SAMPSON** If I am angered I will pull my sword out.
GREGORY Ay, while you live, draw your neck out o' the collar.	**GREGORY** Yes, but you should try to avoid conflict.
SAMPSON I strike quickly, being moved.	**SAMPSON:** If I am angered I will attack quickly.
GREGORY But thou art not quickly moved to strike.	**GREGORY:** But you don't quickly get angry.
SAMPSON A dog of the house of Montague moves me.	**SAMPSON:** Those idiot Montagues make me angry.
GREGORY To move is to stir; and to be valiant is to stand: therefore, if thou art moved, thou runn'st away.	**GREGORY:** By being moved to action you are backing off and running away. Brave people just stand still and unafraid.
SAMPSON A dog of that house shall move me to stand: I will take the wall of any man or maid of Montague's.	**SAMPSON:** Any of those stupid Montagues will make me fight. I will treat the Montagues as inferior by taking the wall with their men *(taking the superior position when walking down the street).*
GREGORY That shows thee a weak slave; for the weakest goes to the wall.	**GREGORY:** Well then you are weak, as only weak people go to the wall *(this is a pun on how women are pushed up against walls to have sex).*

SAMPSON True; and therefore women, being the weaker vessels, are ever thrust to the wall: therefore I will push Montague's men from the wall, and thrust his maids to the wall.	**SAMPSON:** You're right; women are always being pushed up against the wall, so I will push Montague's men away from the wall and have sex with his women up against it.
GREGORY The quarrel is between our masters and us their men.	**GREGORY:** The argument is between the men of the families- leave the women out of it.
SAMPSON 'Tis all one, I will show myself a tyrant: when I have fought with the men, I will be cruel with the maids, and cut off their heads.	**SAMPSON** It's all the same - I will fight the men and take the virginity of the women.
GREGORY The heads of the maids?	**GREGORY** Take their lives?
SAMPSON Ay, the heads of the maids, or their maidenheads; take it in what sense thou wilt.	**SAMPSON** Yes, their lives or their virginities - take it how you like it.
GREGORY They must take it in sense that feel it.	**GREGORY** It's the women who must take it.
SAMPSON Me they shall feel while I am able to stand: and 'tis known I am a pretty piece of flesh.	**SAMPSON** The women will feel me for as long as I can keep it up. Everyone knows I am well endowed.
GREGORY 'Tis well thou art not fish; if thou hadst, thou hadst been poor John. Draw thy tool! here comes two of the house of the Montagues.	**GREGORY** It's a good job you are not a fish. If you were you would be salted and dried. Get your weapon out! Here come two of the Montagues.
SAMPSON My naked weapon is out: quarrel, I will back thee.	**SAMPSON** My sword is out: fight, I will back you up.
GREGORY How! turn thy back and run?	**GREGORY** How! By running away?
SAMPSON Fear me not.	**SAMPSON** Don't worry about me.
GREGORY No, marry; I fear thee!	**GREGORY** No, I am afraid of you!

SAMPSON Let us take the law of our sides; let them begin.	**SAMPSON** Let's keep it lawful; let's provoke them to start the fight so that we can't be blamed for it.
GREGORY I will frown as I pass by, and let them take it as they list.	**GREGORY** I will pull a stupid face at them as they go by, and let's see how they react.
SAMPSON Nay, as they dare. I will bite my thumb at them; which is a disgrace to them, if they bear it.	**SAMPSON** No, I will bite my thumb at them *(a modern equivalent would be somewhere along the lines of 'sticking your fingers up' at someone, although this original insult is very sexual)*. If they don't react then it will show them up.
Enter ABRAHAM and BALTHASAR	*Enter ABRAHAM and BALTHASAR*
ABRAHAM Do you bite your thumb at us, sir?	**ABRAHAM** Are you making an insulting gesture at me?
SAMPSON I do bite my thumb, sir.	**SAMPSON** I am making a gesture.
ABRAHAM Do you bite your thumb at us, sir?	**ABRAHAM** Is it directed at us?
SAMPSON [Aside to GREGORY] Is the law of our side, if I say ay?	**SAMPSON** (quietly to Gregory) If I say 'yes' will we still be able to escape blame if this ends up in a fight?
GREGORY No.	**GREGORY** No.
SAMPSON No, sir, I do not bite my thumb at you, sir, but I bite my thumb, sir.	**SAMPSON** No. I am making a gesture but it is not directed at you.
GREGORY Do you quarrel, sir?	**GREGORY** Do you want a fight?
ABRAHAM Quarrel sir! no, sir.	**ABRAHAM** Fight! No.
SAMPSON If you do, sir, I am for you: I serve as good a man as you.	**SAMPSON** I am quite happy to fight if you want to - my boss is just as great as yours.

ABRAHAM No better.	**ABRAHAM** No better.
SAMPSON Well, sir.	**SAMPSON** Well.
GREGORY Say 'better:' here comes one of my master's kinsmen.	**GREGORY** Say our boss is better; here comes one of our men.
SAMPSON Yes, better, sir.	**SAMPSON** Our boss is better than yours.
ABRAHAM You lie.	**ABRAHAM** You are a liar.
SAMPSON Draw, if you be men. Gregory, remember thy swashing blow.	**SAMPSON** Pull your sword out and fight if you are brave enough. Gregory, remember your special sword attack.
They fight	*They fight.*
Enter BENVOLIO	*Enter BENVOLIO*
BENVOLIO Part, fools! Put up your swords; you know not what you do.	**BENVOLIO** Break it up, idiots! Put your swords away; you don't know what you are doing.
Beats down their swords	*Hits their swords down with his own.*
Enter TYBALT	*Enter TYBALT.*
TYBALT What, art thou drawn among these heartless hinds? Turn thee, Benvolio, look upon thy death.	**TYBALT** You've got your sword out among these girly weaklings? Turn around, Benvolio, I am going to kill you.
BENVOLIO I do but keep the peace: put up thy sword, Or manage it to part these men with me.	**BENVOLIO** I am just trying to calm it down: put your sword away, or use it split these men up.
TYBALT What, drawn, and talk of peace! I hate the word, As I hate hell, all Montagues, and thee: Have at thee, coward!	**TYBALT** You have your sword out and you're talking about peace! I hate the word, just like I hate hell, the Montague family and you: take this!
They fight	*They fight*

Enter, several of both houses, who join the fray; then enter Citizens, with clubs	*Enter men from both sides who join the fight, then Citizens of Verona who also join in*
First Citizen Clubs, bills, and partisans! strike! beat them down! Down with the Capulets! down with the Montagues!	**First Citizen** Hit them with whatever you've got! Down with the Capulets! Down with the Montagues!
Enter CAPULET in his gown, and LADY CAPULET	*Enter CAPULET and his wife.*
CAPULET What noise is this? Give me my long sword, ho!	**CAPULET** What is happening? Give me my sword!
LADY CAPULET A crutch, a crutch! why call you for a sword?	**LADY CAPULET** A sword? You need a crutch old man!
CAPULET My sword, I say! Old Montague is come, And flourishes his blade in spite of me.	**CAPULET** I want my sword! Old Montague is here and has his sword out too.
Enter MONTAGUE and LADY MONTAGUE	*Enter Montague and his wife.*
MONTAGUE Thou villain Capulet,--Hold me not, let me go.	**MONTAGUE** You criminal Capulet - don't hold me back.
LADY MONTAGUE Thou shalt not stir a foot to seek a foe.	**LADY MONTAGUE** You will not get involved in this fight.
Enter PRINCE, with Attendants	*Enter PRINCE, with Attendants*
PRINCE Rebellious subjects, enemies to peace, Profaners of this neighbour-stained steel,-- Will they not hear? What, ho! you men, you beasts, That quench the fire of your pernicious rage With purple fountains issuing from your veins, On pain of torture, from those bloody hands Throw your mistemper'd weapons to the ground, And hear the sentence of your moved prince. Three civil brawls, bred of an airy word, By thee, old Capulet, and Montague, Have thrice disturb'd the quiet of our streets, And made Verona's ancient citizens Cast by their grave beseeming ornaments, To wield old partisans, in hands as old,	**PRINCE** Defiant subjects, haters of peace, Disrespectful misusers of weapons,-- Are they not listening? You wild animals, That put out the fire of your anger with blood pouring out of you, Unless you want to be tortured, drop your weapons And I will tell you my decision on how to deal with you. Three times you've disrupted our city with big fights, started by a silly comment from you Capulet, and you Montague. Three times you've disrupted the quiet streets, And made the city's old people, Pull out their old swords (which are now just ornaments), To fight, in their old hands,

Canker'd with peace, to part your canker'd hate:	Their old swords are rusted because they've not needed to use them for so long, and now they use them to stop the hate which has ruined your families.
If ever you disturb our streets again,	If you ever have another fight in public,
Your lives shall pay the forfeit of the peace.	You will be killed.
For this time, all the rest depart away:	For now, everyone else go away:
You Capulet; shall go along with me:	Capulet come with me:
And, Montague, come you this afternoon,	Montague, come and see me this afternoon,
To know our further pleasure in this case,	To find out what I want to do with you,
To old Free-town, our common judgment-place.	To Free-town, our court-house.
Once more, on pain of death, all men depart.	Again, everyone leave, else you will be put to death.

Exeunt all but MONTAGUE, LADY MONTAGUE, and BENVOLIO	*Exit all but Montague, his wife and Benvolio*

MONTAGUE

Who set this ancient quarrel new abroach?	Who re-started this old battle?
Speak, nephew, were you by when it began?	Tell me, nephew, were you here when it started?

BENVOLIO

Here were the servants of your adversary,	Capulet's servants were here,
And yours, close fighting ere I did approach:	And your servants too, fighting when I arrived:
I drew to part them: in the instant came	I pulled my sword out to stop them fighting: then hot-headed Tybalt arrived with his sword out.
The fiery Tybalt, with his sword prepared,	
Which, as he breathed defiance to my ears,	He was saying nasty things to me,
He swung about his head and cut the winds,	He swished his sword around in the air,
Who nothing hurt withal hiss'd him in scorn:	His sword hit nothing but the air which made a hissing noise as he hit it:
While we were interchanging thrusts and blows,	While we were fighting;
Came more and more and fought on part and part,	More and more people turned up and started fighting too,
Till the prince came, who parted either part.	Until the prince arrived, and he stopped it.

LADY MONTAGUE

O, where is Romeo? saw you him to-day?	Where is Romeo? Have you seen him today?
Right glad I am he was not at this fray.	I am glad he wasn't involved in this fight.

BENVOLIO

Madam, an hour before the worshipp'd sun	Madam, an hour before sunrise,
Peer'd forth the golden window of the east,	
A troubled mind drave me to walk abroad;	I was stressed out and decided to go for a walk;
Where, underneath the grove of sycamore	Where, under a tree

That westward rooteth from the city's side,
So early walking did I see your son:
Towards him I made, but he was ware of me
And stole into the covert of the wood:
I, measuring his affections by my own,
That most are busied when they're most alone,
Pursued my humour not pursuing his,
And gladly shunn'd who gladly fled from me.

MONTAGUE
Many a morning hath he there been seen,
With tears augmenting the fresh morning dew.
Adding to clouds more clouds with his deep sighs;

But all so soon as the all-cheering sun
Should in the furthest east begin to draw
The shady curtains from Aurora's bed,
Away from the light steals home my heavy son,

And private in his chamber pens himself,
Shuts up his windows, locks far daylight out
And makes himself an artificial night:
Black and portentous must this humour prove,
Unless good counsel may the cause remove.

BENVOLIO
My noble uncle, do you know the cause?

MONTAGUE
I neither know it nor can learn of him.

BENVOLIO
Have you importuned him by any means?

MONTAGUE
Both by myself and many other friends:
But he, his own affections' counsellor,
Is to himself--I will not say how true--
But to himself so secret and so close,
So far from sounding and discovery,
As is the bud bit with an envious worm,
Ere he can spread his sweet leaves to the air,
Or dedicate his beauty to the sun.
Could we but learn from whence his sorrows grow.
We would as willingly give cure as know.

Enter ROMEO

BENVOLIO
See, where he comes: so please you, step aside;

At the west of the city
I saw Romeo:
I went towards him but he saw me
And ran off into the woods:
I, thinking he was like me,
Who likes to think of my own,
Did not chase after him,
But let him run away.

MONTAGUE
We have seen him there many mornings,
Crying.
Adding to the clouds with his unhappy
sighs;
But as soon as the sun
Comes up

He runs home,

And locks himself in his room,
Shuts the windows to block out the sun
And makes it look like night in there:
This seems to be worryingly significant,
Unless someone can work out what is
wrong and help him out.

BENVOLIO
Good uncle, do you know why he is upset?

MONTAGUE
I don't know and he won't tell me.

BENVOLIO:
Have you tried to find out?

MONTAGUE:
I have, and many friends have too:
But he keeps himself to himself,

Romeo is like a flower which won't open
up to the world because it has been
poisoned before it can truly live,
If we could learn why he is sad.
We could try and help him get better.

Enter Romeo

BENVOLIO
Here he comes: please go away;

I'll know his grievance, or be much denied.

MONTAGUE
I would thou wert so happy by thy stay,
To hear true shrift. Come, madam, let's away.

Exeunt MONTAGUE and LADY MONTAGUE

BENVOLIO
Good-morrow, cousin.

ROMEO
Is the day so young?

BENVOLIO
But new struck nine.

ROMEO
Ay me! sad hours seem long.
Was that my father that went hence so fast?

BENVOLIO
It was. What sadness lengthens Romeo's hours?

ROMEO
Not having that, which, having, makes them short.

BENVOLIO
In love?

ROMEO
Out--

BENVOLIO
Of love?

ROMEO
Out of her favour, where I am in love.

BENVOLIO
Alas, that love, so gentle in his view,
Should be so tyrannous and rough in proof!

ROMEO
Alas, that love, whose view is muffled still,

Should, without eyes, see pathways to his will!

I'll find out why he is sad.

MONTAGUE:
I hope you find out why he is so upset.
Come on wife, let's go.

Exit Montague and his wife.

BENVOLIO
Good morning, cousin.

ROMEO
Is it still so early as to be morning?

BENVOLIO
It's just past nine AM.

ROMEO
Time goes slowly when you are sad.
Was that my dad who just ran off?

BENVOLIO
Yes it was. What sad thing makes your
time go so slowly?

ROMEO
Not having the thing that, if I had it, would
make time go quickly.

BENVOLIO
Are you in love?

ROMEO
Out—

BENVOLIO
Of love?

ROMEO
She doesn't love me, the one who I love.

BENVOLIO
Shame, love looks so simple
But when you are in love it is so rough!

ROMEO
Shame, that love which is supposed to be
blind,
Even without eyes can make you do
whatever it likes!

Where shall we dine? O me! What fray was here?	Where shall we go and eat? Oh no! You've been in a fight.
Yet tell me not, for I have heard it all. Here's much to do with hate, but more with love.	Don't even tell me, I've heard it all before. This fight is to do with hating, but also loving.
Why, then, O brawling love! O loving hate! O any thing, of nothing first create! O heavy lightness! serious vanity! Mis-shapen chaos of well-seeming forms! Feather of lead, bright smoke, cold fire, sick health! Still-waking sleep, that is not what it is! This love feel I, that feel no love in this.	Why, hate filled love! Oh love filled hate! Love that comes from nothing! Depressing happiness! Serious stupidity! Beautiful things mixed up in chaos! Light and heavy, hot and cold, sick and well! Being awake and asleep, that's not what love is! I feel love, but no-one loves me.
Dost thou not laugh?	Are you laughing?
BENVOLIO No, coz, I rather weep.	**BENVOLIO** No, cousin. I am crying.
ROMEO Good heart, at what?	**ROMEO** Good man, what are you crying at?
BENVOLIO At thy good heart's oppression.	**BENVOLIO** At how depressed you are feeling.
ROMEO Why, such is love's transgression. Griefs of mine own lie heavy in my breast, Which thou wilt propagate, to have it prest	**ROMEO** That is what love is like. I feel very unhappy. And you will add to it by making me feel sympathy
With more of thine: this love that thou hast shown	For your own unhappiness: the love you have shown me
Doth add more grief to too much of mine own. Love is a smoke raised with the fume of sighs;	Makes me even sadder than I already was. Love is like smoke made up of unhappy sighs;
Being purged, a fire sparkling in lovers' eyes; Being vex'd a sea nourish'd with lovers' tears:	A fire which burns in your lovers' eyes; Unhappiness in love can fill a sea with tears:
What is it else? a madness most discreet,	What else is love? It's madness most intelligent.
A choking gall and a preserving sweet. Farewell, my coz.	A sweet which you choke on. Goodbye cousin.
BENVOLIO Soft! I will go along; An if you leave me so, you do me wrong.	**BENVOLIO** Hang on! I will come with you; And if you leave me that's unfair.
ROMEO Tut, I have lost myself; I am not here; This is not Romeo, he's some other where.	**ROMEO** I am lost; I am not here; This isn't the real Romeo, he is somewhere else.

Original	Modern
BENVOLIO Tell me in sadness, who is that you love.	**BENVOLIO** Tell me, who is it that you love?
ROMEO What, shall I groan and tell thee?	**ROMEO** Shall I groan and tell you?
BENVOLIO Groan! why, no. But sadly tell me who.	**BENVOLIO** No don't groan. Just tell me who it is.
ROMEO Bid a sick man in sadness make his will: Ah, word ill urged to one that is so ill! In sadness, cousin, I do love a woman.	**ROMEO** Tell a sick man to make his will: It would not help the situation. Seriously cousin, I love a woman.
BENVOLIO I aim'd so near, when I supposed you loved.	**BENVOLIO** I was right then, when I guessed you were in love.
ROMEO A right good mark-man! And she's fair I love.	**ROMEO** A good guess! And she is beautiful.
BENVOLIO A right fair mark, fair coz, is soonest hit.	**BENVOLIO** Beautiful women fall in love quickly.
ROMEO Well, in that hit you miss: she'll not be hit With Cupid's arrow; she hath Dian's wit; And, in strong proof of chastity well arm'd, From love's weak childish bow she lives unharm'd. She will not stay the siege of loving terms, Nor bide the encounter of assailing eyes, Nor ope her lap to saint-seducing gold: O, she is rich in beauty, only poor, That when she dies with beauty dies her store.	**ROMEO** Well you are wrong there: she doesn't want to fall in love; she's not into sleeping around; And will not have sex with me, She isn't charmed by my childish love for her, She will not listen to my loving words, Or let me look at her with admiring eyes, Or let me have sex with her: She is pretty but poor, When she dies her beauty will die with her.
BENVOLIO Then she hath sworn that she will still live chaste?	**BENVOLIO** Has she taken an oath to remain a virgin?
ROMEO She hath, and in that sparing makes huge waste, For beauty starved with her severity Cuts beauty off from all posterity. She is too fair, too wise, wisely too fair, To merit bliss by making me despair: She hath forsworn to love, and in that vow Do I live dead that live to tell it now.	**ROMEO** She has, and that is a massive waste, Because she is so beautiful and will never pass that beauty onto her own children. She is too pretty and clever, To be blessed by making me so upset: She has made a vow never to fall in love, and because of that promise I am dead inside.

BENVOLIO Be ruled by me, forget to think of her.	**BENVOLIO** Let me tell you what to do: forget her!
ROMEO O, teach me how I should forget to think.	**ROMEO** Teach me how to forget.
BENVOLIO By giving liberty unto thine eyes; Examine other beauties.	**BENVOLIO** By letting your eyes; Look at other beautiful women.
ROMEO 'Tis the way To call hers exquisite, in question more: These happy masks that kiss fair ladies' brows Being black put us in mind they hide the fair; He that is strucken blind cannot forget The precious treasure of his eyesight lost: Show me a mistress that is passing fair, What doth her beauty serve, but as a note Where I may read who pass'd that passing fair? Farewell: thou canst not teach me to forget.	**ROMEO** That is the way To make me think she is even more beautiful: Masks on women's faces Which are black, make us just wonder what their faces are like underneath; A man who goes blind cannot forget What it was like to see before he lost his sight: Show me a fairly pretty woman, Her love is like a letter which tells me Where to find a real beauty. Goodbye: you can't make me forget this woman.
BENVOLIO I'll pay that doctrine, or else die in debt.	**BENVOLIO** I will make you forget, even if I die before having achieved it.
Exeunt	*Exit*

ORIGINAL TEXT	MODERN TEXT
A street. Enter CAPULET, PARIS, and Servant	*A street. Enter CAPULET, PARIS, and Servant*
CAPULET But Montague is bound as well as I, In penalty alike; and 'tis not hard, I think, For men so old as we to keep the peace.	**CAPULET** But Montague is stuck like I am, In a similar punishment; and it's easy, I think, For old men like the two of us to be friends.
PARIS Of honourable reckoning are you both; And pity 'tis you lived at odds so long. But now, my lord, what say you to my suit?	**PARIS** You are both good men; And it's a shame you were enemies for so long. But anyway, what do you say about my offer?
CAPULET But saying o'er what I have said before: My child is yet a stranger in the world; She hath not seen the change of fourteen years, Let two more summers wither in their pride, Ere we may think her ripe to be a bride.	**CAPULET** Just the same as I told you before: My child is young; She is not even yet fourteen years old, Let her get a couple of years older, Before she is ready to marry.
PARIS Younger than she are happy mothers made.	**PARIS** Girls younger than her have had children of their own.
CAPULET And too soon marr'd are those so early made. The earth hath swallow'd all my hopes but she, She is the hopeful lady of my earth: But woo her, gentle Paris, get her heart, My will to her consent is but a part; An she agree, within her scope of choice Lies my consent and fair according voice. This night I hold an old accustom'd feast, Whereto I have invited many a guest, Such as I love; and you, among the store, One more, most welcome, makes my number more. At my poor house look to behold this night	**CAPULET** And those young girls have their lives ruined. All of my hope has gone apart from her, She is so important to me: But seek her affection, Paris, make her fall in love with you, Me saying you can marry her is only part of it; If she chooses to marry you I will let it happen. Tonight I am holding a party, Where I've invited many people to come, People I love; and you are invited, One extra is most welcome. Come to my house tonight

Earth-treading stars that make dark heaven light:	Stars will be there:
Such comfort as do lusty young men feel	Men love to see beautiful women.
When well-apparell'd April on the heel	
Of limping winter treads, even such delight	
Among fresh female buds shall you this night	You will see so many pretty women tonight
	Come to my house; take a look around
Inherit at my house; hear all, all see,	And see who you like:
And like her most whose merit most shall be:	When you've seen lots of women,
Which on more view, of many mine being one	my daughter may not seem so important.
May stand in number, though in reckoning none,	Come with me.
Come, go with me.	

To Servant, giving a paper   (To a servant, giving him a paper)

Go, sirrah, trudge about / Go on, walk around
Through fair Verona; find those persons out / Through Verona; find the people
Whose names are written there, and to them say, / on this guest list, and tell them,
My house and welcome on their pleasure stay. / Me and my house welcome them tonight.

Exeunt CAPULET and PARIS   *Exit CAPULET and PARIS*

Servant   **Servant**

Find them out whose names are written here! It is written, that the shoemaker should meddle with his yard, and the tailor with his last, the fisher with his pencil, and the painter with his nets; but I am sent to find those persons whose names are here writ, and can never find what names the writing person hath here writ. I must to the learned.--In good time.

Find the names written here! It is written that people should try out different things but I am sent to find these people written here and I cannot even read! I must find someone who can read so they can help me.

Enter BENVOLIO and ROMEO   *Enter BENVOLIO and ROMEO*

BENVOLIO   **BENVOLIO**

Tut, man, one fire burns out another's burning,

Mate, you can put one fire out by starting another,

One pain is lessen'd by another's anguish;
Turn giddy, and be holp by backward turning;

We forget our pain when hurt again;
If you get dizzy, you can spin back round the other way and stop the dizziness.

One desperate grief cures with another's languish:
Take thou some new infection to thy eye,
And the rank poison of the old will die.

Focus on some new poison
And the old poison you were looking at will go away.

ROMEO   **ROMEO**

Your plaintain-leaf is excellent for that.   Your sticking plaster is good for that.

BENVOLIO   **BENVOLIO**

For what, I pray thee?   For what?

ROMEO
For your broken shin.

BENVOLIO
Why, Romeo, art thou mad?

ROMEO
Not mad, but bound more than a mad-man is;

Shut up in prison, kept without my food,
Whipp'd and tormented and--God-den, good fellow.

Servant
God gi' god-den. I pray, sir, can you read?

ROMEO
Ay, mine own fortune in my misery.

Servant
Perhaps you have learned it without book: but, I
pray, can you read any thing you see?

ROMEO
Ay, if I know the letters and the language.

Servant
Ye say honestly: rest you merry!

ROMEO
Stay, fellow; I can read.

Reads

'Signior Martino and his wife and daughters;
County Anselme and his beauteous sisters; the lady
widow of Vitravio; Signior Placentio and his lovely
nieces; Mercutio and his brother Valentine; mine
uncle Capulet, his wife and daughters; my fair niece
Rosaline; Livia; Signior Valentio and his cousin

Tybalt, Lucio and the lively Helena.' A fair
assembly: whither should they come?

Servant
Up.

ROMEO
For your broken shin. (A plaintain leaf was
a medical plaster of its day. Here Romeo is
saying that a plaster cannot be used to
mend a broken bone).

BENVOLIO
Romeo are you mad?

ROMEO
Not mad, but tied up more than a mad-
man is;
Locked up, starved, abused and tortured.
Hello friend.

Servant
Hello. Can you read?

ROMEO
Yes, I can read my own fortune and it's
bad.

Servant
You may have learned to do that without
reading: can you read words?

ROMEO
Yes, if I know the language.

Servant
That's the truth. Have a good day!

ROMEO
Stop, friend; I can read.

Reads

'Mr Martino and his wife and daughters;
County Anselme and his beautiful sisters;
the widow of Vitravio, Mr Placentio and
his nieces; Mercutio and his brother
Valentine; my uncle Capulet, his wive and
daughters; my lovely niece Rosaline; Livia;
Mr Valentino and his cousin
Tybalt, Lucio and the lively Helena.' A
good group: where should they go?

Servant
Up.

ROMEO
Whither?

Servant
To supper; to our house.

ROMEO
Whose house?

Servant
My master's.

ROMEO
Indeed, I should have ask'd you that before.

Servant
Now I'll tell you without asking: my master is the great rich Capulet; and if you be not of the house

of Montagues, I pray, come and crush a cup of wine.

Rest you merry!

Exit

BENVOLIO
At this same ancient feast of Capulet's
Sups the fair Rosaline whom thou so lovest,

With all the admired beauties of Verona:

Go thither; and, with unattainted eye,
Compare her face with some that I shall show,

And I will make thee think thy swan a crow.

ROMEO
When the devout religion of mine eye
Maintains such falsehood, then turn tears to fires;

And these, who often drown'd could never die,
Transparent heretics, be burnt for liars!
One fairer than my love! the all-seeing sun

Ne'er saw her match since first the world begun.

ROMEO
Where?

Servant
To eat supper; at our house.

ROMEO
Whose house?

Servant
My boss's.

ROMEO
Obviously, I should have asked that before.

Servant
Now I will tell you without you even asking: my boss is the fantastic rich Capulet; and if you are not one of the Montague family, come and have a drink at the party yourself.
Have a nice day!

Exit

BENVOLIO
At this party of Capulet's
Eats the lovely Rosaline who you are in love with,
Along with all the pretty women of the city.
Go there; and objectively,
Compare her to some other women I will show you,
And I will make you think Rosaline is ugly.

ROMEO
When my eyes
Lie to me like this, then let my tears turn to fire;
And these eyes which often cry,
Should be burnt up for lying!
One more lovely than Rosaline! The sun itself
Never saw anyone as beautiful as her since the world began.

BENVOLIO Tut, you saw her fair, none else being by, Herself poised with herself in either eye: But in that crystal scales let there be weigh'd Your lady's love against some other maid That I will show you shining at this feast, And she shall scant show well that now shows best. **ROMEO** I'll go along, no such sight to be shown, But to rejoice in splendor of mine own. *Exeunt*	**BENVOLIO** You thought she was pretty, because no-one else was there, You just had her to look at: But if you compare her To some other pretty women That I will show you at the party, She will not look so impressive. **ROMEO** I will come along, not to see these other women, But to enjoy looking at Rosaline. Exit

ORIGINAL TEXT	MODERN TRANSLATION
A room in Capulet's house.	A room in Capulet's house.
Enter LADY CAPULET and Nurse	*Enter Lady Capulet and Nurse.*
LADY CAPULET Nurse, where's my daughter? call her forth to me.	**LADY CAPULET** Nurse, where is my daughter? Call her to come to me.
Nurse Now, by my maidenhead, at twelve year old, I bade her come. What, lamb! what, ladybird! God forbid! Where's this girl? What, Juliet!	**Nurse** I swear by the fact I was a virgin at the age of twelve, I already told her to come. Where is she? Juliet!
Enter JULIET	ENTER JULIET
JULIET How now! who calls?	**JULIET** What? Who is calling?
Nurse Your mother.	**Nurse** Your mother.
JULIET Madam, I am here. What is your will?	**JULIET** Woman, I am here. What do you want?
LADY CAPULET This is the matter:--Nurse, give leave awhile, We must talk in secret:--nurse, come back again; I have remember'd me, thou's hear our counsel. Thou know'st my daughter's of a pretty age.	**LADY CAPULET** This is the issue:--Nurse, leave us alone for a bit, We must have a secret chat:--nurse, come back again; You can hear out secrets. You know my daughter is of a young age.
Nurse Faith, I can tell her age unto an hour.	**Nurse** Yes, I know her age exactly.
LADY CAPULET She's not fourteen.	**LADY CAPULET** She isn't yet fourteen.
Nurse I'll lay fourteen of my teeth,-- And yet, to my teeth be it spoken, I have but four-- She is not fourteen. How long is it now To Lammas-tide?	**Nurse** I would bet with fourteen of my teeth,-- Except I only have four of them-- She is not fourteen. How long is it until Augst first?

LADY CAPULET

A fortnight and odd days.

Nurse

Even or odd, of all days in the year,
Come Lammas-eve at night shall she be fourteen.
Susan and she--God rest all Christian souls!--
Were of an age: well, Susan is with God;

She was too good for me: but, as I said,

On Lammas-eve at night shall she be fourteen;
That shall she, marry; I remember it well.
'Tis since the earthquake now eleven years;

And she was wean'd,--I never shall forget it,--

Of all the days of the year, upon that day:

For I had then laid wormwood to my dug,
Sitting in the sun under the dove-house wall;

My lord and you were then at Mantua:--
Nay, I do bear a brain:--but, as I said,

When it did taste the wormwood on the nipple
Of my dug and felt it bitter, pretty fool,
To see it tetchy and fall out with the dug!
Shake quoth the dove-house: 'twas no need, I trow,

To bid me trudge:
And since that time it is eleven years;
For then she could stand alone; nay, by the rood,
She could have run and waddled all about;
For even the day before, she broke her brow:
And then my husband--God be with his soul!
A' was a merry man--took up the child:
'Yea,' quoth he, 'dost thou fall upon thy face?
Thou wilt fall backward when thou hast more wit;

Wilt thou not, Jule?' and, by my holidame,
The pretty wretch left crying and said 'Ay.'

To see, now, how a jest shall come about!
I warrant, an I should live a thousand years,

I never should forget it: 'Wilt thou not, Jule?' quoth he;
And, pretty fool, it stinted and said 'Ay.'

LADY CAPULET

About two weeks.

Nurse

Close or not close,
On August first she shall be fourteen.
Susan-- God rest her departed soul!
Was about the age: well, Susan is dead now;
She was too good to remain on earth: but, as I was saying,
On August first she shall be fourteen;
That she will; I can remember it very well.
Eleven years have passed since the earthquake;
And she stopped breastfeeding--I will never forget it,
Of all the days to stop, she stopped on that day:
For I had put a bitter herb on my nipple,
Sitting in the sun under the dove-house wall;
You and Lord Capulet were at Mantua:
What a memory I have: but, as I was saying,
When she tasted the herb on my nipple
And tasted that it was bitter
She fell out of love with my breast!
Then the earthquake shook the dove-house: there was no need,
To tell me to get out:
And since then it's been eleven years;
She could stand up on her own,
She could run around.
Even the day before, she cut her forehead:
And my husband, also dearly departed,
He was a happy man--he picked her up,
"oh" he said "did you fall on your face?"
You will fall backwards when you're a bit older;
Won't you Julie? and, I swear,
The little baby stopped crying and said "yes."
What a joke!
I promise, I could live a thousand more years,
I never will forget it: "Won't you Julie" he said;
And the pretty baby stopped crying and said "Yes".

LADY CAPULET
Enough of this; I pray thee, hold thy peace.

Nurse
Yes, madam: yet I cannot choose but laugh,
To think it should leave crying and say 'Ay.'
And yet, I warrant, it had upon its brow
A bump as big as a young cockerel's stone;
A parlous knock; and it cried bitterly:
'Yea,' quoth my husband, 'fall'st upon thy face?
Thou wilt fall backward when thou comest to age;

Wilt thou not, Jule?' it stinted and said 'Ay.'

JULIET
And stint thou too, I pray thee, nurse, say I.

Nurse
Peace, I have done. God mark thee to his grace!
Thou wast the prettiest babe that e'er I nursed:

An I might live to see thee married once,
I have my wish.

LADY CAPULET
Marry, that 'marry' is the very theme
I came to talk of. Tell me, daughter Juliet,
How stands your disposition to be married?

JULIET
It is an honour that I dream not of.

Nurse
An honour! were not I thine only nurse,

I would say thou hadst suck'd wisdom from thy teat.

LADY CAPULET
Well, think of marriage now; younger than you,

Here in Verona, ladies of esteem,
Are made already mothers: by my count,
I was your mother much upon these years
That you are now a maid. Thus then in brief:
The valiant Paris seeks you for his love.

LADY CAPULET
Enough of this story; be quiet for a bit.

Nurse
Yes, madam: but I can't help but laugh,
To think she stopped crying and said 'yes'.
And yet, I'll bet, upon her forehead
was a huge bump;
A massive knock; and she cried loudly:
'Oh' said my husband, 'fall on your face?
You will fall backwards when you become
a woman'
'Will you not, Jule?' she stopped crying
and said 'yes.'

JULIET
And you stop too, please, nurse, I say.

Nurse
Calm down, I am finished.
You were the prettiest baby I ever
breastfed:
And if I live to see you married,
I shall have my wish.

LADY CAPULET
Marriage is the very topic
I came to talk about. Tell me Juliet,
How do you feel about getting married?

JULIET
It is something special that I do not even
think about.

Nurse
Something special! If I wasn't the only one
who breastfed you,
I would say you had sucked wisdom out of
the nipple.

LADY CAPULET
Well, start thinking about marriage now;
younger than you,
Here in this city, posh ladies,
Already have kids: as I remember,
I gave birth you to around your age
And you are still a virgin. Let me be quick:
Paris wants to marry you.

Nurse

A man, young lady! lady, such a man
As all the world--why, he's a man of wax.

LADY CAPULET

Verona's summer hath not such a flower.

Nurse

Nay, he's a flower; in faith, a very flower.

LADY CAPULET

What say you? can you love the gentleman?
This night you shall behold him at our feast;

Read o'er the volume of young Paris' face,
And find delight writ there with beauty's pen;
Examine every married lineament,
And see how one another lends content
And what obscured in this fair volume lies
Find written in the margent of his eyes.
This precious book of love, this unbound lover,

To beautify him, only lacks a cover:
The fish lives in the sea, and 'tis much pride
For fair without the fair within to hide:

That book in many's eyes doth share the glory,
That in gold clasps locks in the golden story;
So shall you share all that he doth possess,
By having him, making yourself no less.

Nurse

No less! nay, bigger; women grow by men.

LADY CAPULET

Speak briefly, can you like of Paris' love?

JULIET

I'll look to like, if looking liking move:
But no more deep will I endart mine eye
Than your consent gives strength to make it fly.

Enter a Servant

Servant

Madam, the guests are come, supper served up, you
called, my young lady asked for, the nurse cursed in
the pantry, and every thing in extremity. I must
hence to wait; I beseech you, follow straight.

Nurse

He's an amazing man! He's so stunning it's
like he is a sculpture.

LADY CAPULET

The city's summer isn't as hot as he is!

Nurse

No, he's an amazing flower.

LADY CAPULET

What do you think? Can you love him?
Tonight he is coming to the party at our
house;
Have a good look at his face;
And see how beautiful he is;
Look at every bit of his features,
And see how they complement each other
And what you can't work out
Find it in his eyes.
This amazing man is like a book without a
cover,
To perfect him he needs that cover:
The fish live in the sea, and that is right,
It would be wrong for you to hide from a
great man like him:
Paris is admired by many,

And you will be too,
If you marry him.

Nurse

You will become even more perfect if you
marry him.

LADY CAPULET

Tell me quickly, can you fall in love with
him?

JULIET

I'll try to,
But I won't fall any more deeply in love
Than you let me.

Enter a servant

Servant

Madam, the guests are here, food is
dished up, you are wanted, Juliet is
wanted, people are moaning about the
nurse.

	Please, come with me.
LADY CAPULET We follow thee.	**LADY CAPULET** We are coming.
Exit Servant	*Exit Servant*
Juliet, the county stays.	Juliet, Paris is waiting for you.
Nurse Go, girl, seek happy nights to happy days.	**Nurse** Go on, girl. Look for a man who will give you happy nights.
Exeunt	Exit

Act 1 Scene 4

ORIGINAL TEXT	MODERN TRANSLATION
A street.	A street.
Enter ROMEO, MERCUTIO, BENVOLIO, with five or six Maskers, Torch-bearers, and others	Enter ROMEO, MERCUTIO, BENVOLIO, with five or six Masker, Torch-bearers, and others
ROMEO What, shall this speech be spoke for our excuse? Or shall we on without a apology?	**ROMEO** What excuse shall we give for being here? Or shall we just go in without an explanation?
BENVOLIO The date is out of such prolixity: We'll have no Cupid hoodwink'd with a scarf, Bearing a Tartar's painted bow of lath, Scaring the ladies like a crow-keeper; Nor no without-book prologue, faintly spoke After the prompter, for our entrance: But let them measure us by what they will; We'll measure them a measure, and be gone.	**BENVOLIO** It's unfashionable to give long explanations: We won't have our dance introduced by having someone dress up as characters, Carrying a bow, Scaring the ladies. And we're not going to have a long speech planned, When we arrive: But let them think of us what they like: We'll have a bit of a dance, then leave.
ROMEO Give me a torch: I am not for this ambling; Being but heavy, I will bear the light.	**ROMEO** Give me a light: I don't want to dance at this party; I'm too depressed, so I will be the one who carries the light.
MERCUTIO Nay, gentle Romeo, we must have you dance.	**MERCUTIO** No, Romeo, you must dance.
ROMEO Not I, believe me: you have dancing shoes With nimble soles: I have a soul of lead So stakes me to the ground I cannot move.	**ROMEO** Not me: you are the one with dancing shoes on My unhappiness means I cannot move.
MERCUTIO You are a lover; borrow Cupid's wings, And soar with them above a common bound.	**MERCUTIO** You are in love, so borrow the wings of Cupid, and fly with them.
ROMEO I am too sore enpierced with his shaft To soar with his light feathers, and so bound, I cannot bound a pitch above dull woe:	**ROMEO** I am too wounded from Cupid's arrow, To fly, so I am stuck, I cannot move much at all:

Under love's heavy burden do I sink.	Under the sadness of love which weighs me down.
MERCUTIO And, to sink in it, should you burden love; Too great oppression for a tender thing.	**MERCUTIO** And, by sinking, you are pulling love down; Love should not be weighed down.
ROMEO Is love a tender thing? it is too rough, Too rude, too boisterous, and it pricks like thorn.	**ROMEO** Is love tender? It's rough, rude and very painful.
MERCUTIO If love be rough with you, be rough with love; Prick love for pricking, and you beat love down. Give me a case to put my visage in: A visor for a visor! what care I What curious eye doth quote deformities? Here are the beetle brows shall blush for me.	**MERCUTIO** If love is rough, be rough back; Prick love if it pricks you, and beat love down. Give me a mask to cover my face: Another mask to go over that mask! What do I care if people see the real me? This mask will blush for me.
BENVOLIO Come, knock and enter; and no sooner in, But every man betake him to his legs.	**BENVOLIO** Come on, knock the door and go in, As soon as we get in, start dancing.
ROMEO A torch for me: let wantons light of heart Tickle the senseless rushes with their heels, For I am proverb'd with a grandsire phrase; I'll be a candle-holder, and look on. The game was ne'er so fair, and I am done.	**ROMEO** Give me a light: let people who are happy dance Like the old saying goes, you can't lose if you don't play the game; I'll hold the light and watch. It looks like fun.
MERCUTIO Tut, dun's the mouse, the constable's own word: If thou art dun, we'll draw thee from the mire Of this sir-reverence love, wherein thou stick'st Up to the ears. Come, we burn daylight, ho!	**MERCUTIO** You're as gloomy as a policeman: If you are gloomy, we'll pull you out of it Out of love where you are stuck, Up to your ears. Come on, we're wasting time.
ROMEO Nay, that's not so.	**ROMEO** That's not true.
MERCUTIO I mean, sir, in delay We waste our lights in vain, like lamps by day. Take our good meaning, for our judgment sits Five times in that ere once in our five wits.	**MERCUTIO** I mean by delaying going in, We waste our lights, like burning a candle in the daytime, Understand what I mean, rather than try to think of some clever meaning.

ROMEO And we mean well in going to this mask; But 'tis no wit to go.	**ROMEO** We're going to this party with good intentions, But it's not a good idea.
MERCUTIO Why, may one ask?	**MERCUTIO** Why?
ROMEO I dream'd a dream to-night.	**ROMEO** I had a dream tonight.
MERCUTIO And so did I.	**MERCUTIO** Me too.
ROMEO Well, what was yours?	**ROMEO** What was your dream?
MERCUTIO That dreamers often lie.	**MERCUTIO** That dreamers often lie.
ROMEO In bed asleep, while they do dream things true.	**ROMEO** When sleeping in bed, their dreams often come true.
MERCUTIO O, then, I see Queen Mab hath been with you. She is the fairies' midwife, and she comes In shape no bigger than an agate-stone On the fore-finger of an alderman, Drawn with a team of little atomies Athwart men's noses as they lie asleep; Her wagon-spokes made of long spiders' legs, The cover of the wings of grasshoppers, The traces of the smallest spider's web, The collars of the moonshine's watery beams, Her whip of cricket's bone, the lash of film, Her wagoner a small grey-coated gnat, Not so big as a round little worm Prick'd from the lazy finger of a maid; Her chariot is an empty hazel-nut Made by the joiner squirrel or old grub, Time out o' mind the fairies' coachmakers. And in this state she gallops night by night Through lovers' brains, and then they dream of love;	**MERCUTIO** Oh, then I see you've been with Queen Mab. She is midwife for the fairies. And she is very small. She is pulled along by tiny atoms Along sleeping men's noses; In a wagon with wheel spokes made of spider legs, A cover made of grasshopper wings, Harnesses made of tiny bits of spider web, Collars made of moonshine. A whip made of bone, Her driver is a tiny gnat wearing a grey coat, Smaller than the worm Which comes from a lazy girl's finger; Her chariot is a nutshell Made by a squirrel or old grubworm, They've made coaches for fairies for as long as can be remembered. And like this she gallops around every night Through the brains of lovers, and then they dream of love;

O'er courtiers' knees, that dream on court'sies straight,	She rides over the knees of courtiers, who dream of curtsying,
O'er lawyers' fingers, who straight dream on fees,	Over lawyers' fingers, who dream of the money they can make,
O'er ladies ' lips, who straight on kisses dream,	Over ladies' lips, who dream of kissing,
Which oft the angry Mab with blisters plagues,	Often Mab angrily puts blisters on their lips,
Because their breaths with sweetmeats tainted are:	Because their breath stinks:
Sometime she gallops o'er a courtier's nose,	Sometimes she rides over a courtier's nose,
And then dreams he of smelling out a suit;	And he dreams of smelling out a lawsuit;
And sometime comes she with a tithe-pig's tail	And sometimes she comes with a tiny pig's tail
Tickling a parson's nose as a' lies asleep,	Tickling a vicar's nose as he sleep,
Then dreams, he of another benefice:	Then dreams he of a large donation:
Sometime she driveth o'er a soldier's neck,	Sometimes she drives over a soldier's neck,
And then dreams he of cutting foreign throats,	And then he dreams about cutting enemy soldier's throats,
Of breaches, ambuscadoes, Spanish blades,	Of breaking down walls, Spanish swords,
Of healths five-fathom deep; and then anon	Of huge alcoholic drinks; and then
Drums in his ear, at which he starts and wakes,	hears drums in his ear, at which he wakes up,
And being thus frighted swears a prayer or two	And being afraid he prays
And sleeps again. This is that very Mab	And falls asleep again. This is Mab
That plats the manes of horses in the night,	That plaits horses manes in the night,
And bakes the elflocks in foul sluttish hairs,	And makes the tangles hard,
Which once untangled, much misfortune bodes:	so that if untangled it brings a curse on the person who untangles them,
This is the hag, when maids lie on their backs,	She is the hag, when virgins have sex,
That presses them and learns them first to bear,	That teaches them how to take a man and how to have babies:
Making them women of good carriage:	
This is she--	That is her.

ROMEO

Peace, peace, Mercutio, peace!
Thou talk'st of nothing.

MERCUTIO

True, I talk of dreams,
Which are the children of an idle brain,

Begot of nothing but vain fantasy,
Which is as thin of substance as the air
And more inconstant than the wind, who wooes

Even now the frozen bosom of the north,
And, being anger'd, puffs away from thence,

Turning his face to the dew-dropping south.

ROMEO

Enough, enough, Mercutio, please!
You are talking rubbish.

MERCUTIO

True, I talk about dreams,
Which only take place in brains which do nothing,

Dreams are just silly ideas,
Which are made up of nothing
And which change quicker than the wind, which blows

Even now cold from the north,
And then gets angry and,

Blows hot from the south.

BENVOLIO

This wind, you talk of, blows us from ourselves;

Supper is done, and we shall come too late.

ROMEO

I fear, too early: for my mind misgives

Some consequence yet hanging in the stars
Shall bitterly begin his fearful date
With this night's revels and expire the term
Of a despised life closed in my breast
By some vile forfeit of untimely death.
But He, that hath the steerage of my course,
Direct my sail! On, lusty gentlemen.

BENVOLIO

Strike, drum.

Exeunt

BENVOLIO

This wind you are talking about blows us away from our plan;
The food will soon be gone, and we will arrive too late.

ROMEO

I am afraid we will arrive too early, for I fear
Something bad is fated to happen
It shall begin today
With this party and end
In my own death
But whoever is in charge of my life

Take me where you want. Let's go men.

BENVOLIO

Bang the drum.

Exit

Act 1 Scene 5

ORIGINAL TEXT	MODERN TRANSLATION
A hall in Capulet's house.	A hall in Capulet's house.
Musicians waiting. Enter Servingmen with napkins	*Musicians are stood waiting. Waiter enter with napkins.*
First Servant Where's Potpan, that he helps not to take away? He shift a trencher? he scrape a trencher!	**First Servant** Where's Potpan, why isn't he clearing tables? He should be tidying dishes and washing them up!
Second Servant When good manners shall lie all in one or two men's hands and they unwashed too, 'tis a foul thing.	**Second Servant** When there are only one or two good mannered people, And they're dirty too, it's a bad thing.
First Servant Away with the joint-stools, remove the court-cupboard, look to the plate. Good thou, save me a piece of marchpane; and, as thou lovest me, let the porter let in Susan Grindstone and Nell. Antony, and Potpan!	**First Servant** Put the stools away, remove the plates. Save me a piece of marzipan if you love me, let Susan Grindstone and Nell in. Antony, and Potpan!
Second Servant Ay, boy, ready.	**Second Servant** Yes boy I'm ready.
First Servant You are looked for and called for, asked for and sought for, in the great chamber.	**First Servant** You are wanted in the great chamber room.
Second Servant We cannot be here and there too. Cheerly, boys; be brisk awhile, and the longer liver take all.	**Second Servant** We can't be everywhere at once. Cheers, boys; be quick and the oldest take everything.
Enter CAPULET, with JULIET and others of his house, meeting the Guests and Maskers	*Enter CAPULET, JULIET and others, meeting the Guests and Maskers*
CAPULET Welcome, gentlemen! ladies that have their toes Unplagued with corns will have a bout with you. Ah ha, my mistresses! which of you all Will now deny to dance? she that makes dainty,	**CAPULET** Welcome men! Ladies that have toes that are healthy will dance with you. Ha ha, my women! Which of you all Will say no to a dance now? The woman that does,

She, I'll swear, hath corns; am I come near ye now?

Welcome, gentlemen! I have seen the day
That I have worn a visor and could tell
A whispering tale in a fair lady's ear,
Such as would please: 'tis gone, 'tis gone, 'tis gone:
You are welcome, gentlemen! come, musicians,
play.

A hall, a hall! give room! and foot it, girls.

Music plays, and they dance

More light, you knaves; and turn the tables up,

And quench the fire, the room is grown too hot.

Ah, sirrah, this unlook'd-for sport comes well.
Nay, sit, nay, sit, good cousin Capulet;
For you and I are past our dancing days:
How long is't now since last yourself and I
Were in a mask?

Second Capulet
By'r lady, thirty years.

CAPULET
What, man! 'tis not so much, 'tis not so much:
'Tis since the nuptials of Lucentio,
Come pentecost as quickly as it will,
Some five and twenty years; and then we mask'd.

Second Capulet
'Tis more, 'tis more, his son is elder, sir;
His son is thirty.

CAPULET
Will you tell me that?
His son was but a ward two years ago.

ROMEO
[To a Servingman] What lady is that, which doth
enrich the hand
Of yonder knight?

Servant
I know not, sir.

She, I promise, has corns on her feet; am I
right?
Welcome, men! When I was younger
I could wear a mask and tell
A flirtatious story to a woman by
whispering in her ear.
Now those days are gone:
You are welcome, men! Come, musicians,
play.
A hall, make room in the hall! Dance girls.

Music plays, and they dance.

Make it lighter in here, you servants; and
move the tables out of the way,
And cool down the fire, it's too hot in this
room.
Ah, sir, this unexpected fun is great.
No, sit down cousin Capulet;
For you and I are too old to dance:
How long is it now since we were both
masked up at a ball like this?

Second Capulet
Thirty years.

CAPULET
What, man! It's not that long:
It's since Luncentio got married,
Let time fly as fast as it likes,
It's only twenty five years since we were
masked.

Second Capulet
It's more, it's more. His son is older than
that.
His son is thirty.

CAPULET
What are you saying?
His son was still a child a couple of years
ago.

ROMEO
(to a servant) who is that lady,
who holds the hand
of that knight over there?

Servant
I don't know, sir.

ROMEO

O, she doth teach the torches to burn bright!

It seems she hangs upon the cheek of night
Like a rich jewel in an Ethiope's ear;
Beauty too rich for use, for earth too dear!

So shows a snowy dove trooping with crows,
As yonder lady o'er her fellows shows.
The measure done, I'll watch her place of stand,

And, touching hers, make blessed my rude hand.
Did my heart love till now? forswear it, sight!
For I ne'er saw true beauty till this night.

TYBALT

This, by his voice, should be a Montague.

Fetch me my rapier, boy. What dares the slave

Come hither, cover'd with an antic face,
To fleer and scorn at our solemnity?
Now, by the stock and honour of my kin,
To strike him dead, I hold it not a sin.

CAPULET

Why, how now, kinsman! wherefore storm you so?

TYBALT

Uncle, this is a Montague, our foe,
A villain that is hither come in spite,
To scorn at our solemnity this night.

CAPULET

Young Romeo is it?

TYBALT

'Tis he, that villain Romeo.

CAPULET

Content thee, gentle coz, let him alone;
He bears him like a portly gentleman;
And, to say truth, Verona brags of him
To be a virtuous and well-govern'd youth:
I would not for the wealth of all the town
Here in my house do him disparagement:
Therefore be patient, take no note of him:
It is my will, the which if thou respect,
Show a fair presence and put off these frowns,
And ill-beseeming semblance for a feast.

ROMEO

Oh, she shines so brightly she is teaching
the lights how to do it!
She stand out against the night
Like a bright jewel in a black person's ear;
Too beautiful for love, too amazing for
earth!
Like a white bird among black ones,
She stands out among the other women.
When the dance is over, I'll watch where
she stands,
And touch her hand with mine.
Did I ever love until now? No I did not!
I've never seen true beauty until now.

TYBALT

This man, by the sound of his voice, is a
Montague.
Get me my sword, servant. How dare that
slave
come here, with a mask on his face,
To mock us in our celebration?
No, I swear on my family,
I will kill him, and not regret it.

CAPULET

How are you, relative! Where are you
going so angrily?

TYBALT

Uncle, this man is a Montague, our enemy,
A criminal come here to mock us,
To laugh at our seriousness tonight.

CAPULET

Young Romeo is it?

TYBALT

Yes it is, that villain Romeo.

CAPULET

Calm down, cousin, leave him alone;
He is behaving himself,
And the city loves him
As a good and well behaved youth:
I do not want, for anything, for him to be
cast in a bad light in my house:
Be patient, ignore him:
It is my decision, if you respect it,
That you stop looking angry
A bad look for a party.

TYBALT
It fits, when such a villain is a guest:
I'll not endure him.

CAPULET
He shall be endured:
What, goodman boy! I say, he shall: go to;

Am I the master here, or you? go to.
You'll not endure him! God shall mend my soul!
You'll make a mutiny among my guests!
You will set cock-a-hoop! you'll be the man!

TYBALT
Why, uncle, 'tis a shame.

CAPULET
Go to, go to;
You are a saucy boy: is't so, indeed?
This trick may chance to scathe you, I know what:

You must contrary me! marry, 'tis time.
Well said, my hearts! You are a princox; go:

Be quiet, or--More light, more light! For shame!

I'll make you quiet. What, cheerly, my hearts!

TYBALT
Patience perforce with wilful choler meeting
Makes my flesh tremble in their different greeting.
I will withdraw: but this intrusion shall
Now seeming sweet convert to bitter gall.

Exit

ROMEO
[To JULIET] If I profane with my unworthiest hand

This holy shrine, the gentle fine is this:
My lips, two blushing pilgrims, ready stand
To smooth that rough touch with a tender kiss.

JULIET
Good pilgrim, you do wrong your hand too much,

Which mannerly devotion shows in this;

TYBALT
It's the right look when a criminal like him
is here: I won't put up with it.

CAPULET
He will be put up with:
What, little boy! I tell you he shall. Go away.
Am I the boss or you? Go away.
You'll not put up with it! I am in shock!
You'll cause a war among my guests!
You'll cause chaos! It'll be your fault!

TYBALT
Uncle it's a shame.

CAPULET
Go away.
You are a cocky boy, aren't you?
This will come back to haunt you, I know what:
You want to contradict me! It's time
(to others) Well said, my guests! You are an idiot. Go:
Shut up, or--more light in here, more light! How embarrassing.
Or I will make you shut up. Keep having fun my guests.

TYBALT
Being patient whilst so angry
Makes me shake.
I will back off: but this intrusion
Which now seems so good with end badly.

Exit

ROMEO
(to Juliet)   If I show disrespect to a sacred thing by putting my unholy hand,
In your holy hand, the punishment is this:
My two shy lips, like two men on a religious journey, are ready
To kiss you.

JULIET
Good man on a religious journey, you criticise your hand too severely,
What you do is fine;

For saints have hands that pilgrims' hands do touch,	For people on a pilgrimage touch the hands of holy statues,
And palm to palm is holy palmers' kiss.	And putting two hands together is kind of like a kiss.
ROMEO	**ROMEO**
Have not saints lips, and holy palmers too?	Don't saints and pilgrims have lips?
JULIET	**JULIET**
Ay, pilgrim, lips that they must use in prayer.	Yes, pilgrim, lips to use for praying.
ROMEO	**ROMEO**
O, then, dear saint, let lips do what hands do;	Oh then, let my lips do what hands do;
They pray, grant thou, lest faith turn to despair.	Let my lips be pressed against yours, else I will become sad.
JULIET	**JULIET**
Saints do not move, though grant for prayers' sake.	Saints don't move, even when they answer prayers.
ROMEO	**ROMEO**
Then move not, while my prayer's effect I take.	Then don't move, while I kiss you.
Kisses her	*Kisses her*
Thus from my lips, by yours, my sin is purged.	As I put my lips on yours, I am made pure.
JULIET	**JULIET**
Then have my lips the sin that they have took.	Then do my lips now have the impurity from yours?
ROMEO	**ROMEO**
Sin from thy lips? O trespass sweetly urged!	Impurity on your lips? What you say makes me want to do this bad thing again!
Give me my sin again.	Give me my impurity back.
JULIET	**JULIET**
You kiss by the book.	You're an amazing kisser.
Nurse	**Nurse**
Madam, your mother craves a word with you.	Lady, your mum wants to speak to you.
ROMEO	**ROMEO**
What is her mother?	Who is her mum?
Nurse	**Nurse**
Marry, bachelor,	Young man,
Her mother is the lady of the house,	Her mum is the owner of this house,
And a good lady, and a wise and virtuous	A good woman, clever and honest
I nursed her daughter, that you talk'd withal;	I breastfed her daughter, the one you just talked to;

I tell you, he that can lay hold of her
Shall have the chinks.

ROMEO
Is she a Capulet?
O dear account! my life is my foe's debt.

BENVOLIO
Away, begone; the sport is at the best.

ROMEO
Ay, so I fear; the more is my unrest.

CAPULET
Nay, gentlemen, prepare not to be gone;
We have a trifling foolish banquet towards.
Is it e'en so? why, then, I thank you all
I thank you, honest gentlemen; good night.
More torches here! Come on then, let's to bed.

Ah, sirrah, by my fay, it waxes late:
I'll to my rest.

Exeunt all but JULIET and Nurse

JULIET
Come hither, nurse. What is yond gentleman?

Nurse
The son and heir of old Tiberio.

JULIET
What's he that now is going out of door?

Nurse
Marry, that, I think, be young Petrucio.

JULIET
What's he that follows there, that would not dance?

Nurse
I know not.

JULIET
Go ask his name: if he be married.
My grave is like to be my wedding bed.

I tell you, the man that marries her will
become very rich.

ROMEO
Is she from the Capulet family?
Oh what a costly thing! My life is now in
my enemy's hand.

BENVOLIO
Let's go; the fun is at its height.

ROMEO
Yes, I am afraid it is; I am in a mess.

CAPULET
No, men, don't get ready to leave;
We have some pudding coming along.
Is that right? Why then, thank you all,
thank you good men, good night.
Make it lighter here! Come on then, let's
go to bed.
Ah, it's getting late.
I'm off to bed.

Exit all but Juliet and Nurse.

JULIET
Come here, nurse. Who is that man over
there?

Nurse
The son of Tiberio.

JULIET
Who is he that is walking out now?

Nurse
That is young Petrucio.

JULIET
Who is he following, the one who would
not dance?

Nurse
I don't know.

JULIET
Go and find out who he is: if he's married.
I will die a single woman.

Nurse His name is Romeo, and a Montague; The only son of your great enemy.	**Nurse** His name is Romeo, and he's a Montague; The son of your great enemy.
JULIET My only love sprung from my only hate! Too early seen unknown, and known too late! Prodigious birth of love it is to me, That I must love a loathed enemy.	**JULIET** The only one I love comes from the only one I hate! I saw him before I knew it, and now I know it, it's too late! Love is a monster to me, Making me fall in love with my enemy.
Nurse What's this? what's this?	**Nurse** What are you saying?
JULIET A rhyme I learn'd even now Of one I danced withal.	**JULIET** Just a song I learned From someone I danced with at the party.
One calls within 'Juliet.'	*Someone calls 'Juliet.'*
Nurse Anon, anon! Come, let's away; the strangers all are gone.	**Nurse** Right way, right away! Come on, let's go. The guests are all gone.
Exeunt	*Exit*

Act 2 Prologue

ORIGINAL TEXT	MODERN TRANSLATION
PROLOGUE	Prologue
Enter Chorus	*Enter Chorus*
Chorus	**Chorus**
Now old desire doth in his death-bed lie,	Now Romeo's old feelings are dying away,
And young affection gapes to be his heir;	And new love wants to take their place;
That fair for which love groan'd for and would die,	For Rosaline he said he would die,
With tender Juliet match'd, is now not fair.	But compared to Juliet, Rosaline is nothing.
Now Romeo is beloved and loves again,	Now Romeo is newly in love and loved back,
Alike betwitched by the charm of looks,	Both of them fell in love with each other's looks,
But to his foe supposed he must complain,	But this is his enemy he has to talk to,
And she steal love's sweet bait from fearful hooks:	And she's fallen in love with someone she should fear:
Being held a foe, he may not have access	Because he is thought of as an enemy, he may not be able to get near her
To breathe such vows as lovers use to swear;	to say the sorts of things lover says;
And she as much in love, her means much less	And she is in love too, but is even less able
To meet her new-beloved any where:	To go anywhere to see the one she loves;
But passion lends them power, time means, to meet	But their passion gives them power and time to meet
Tempering extremities with extreme sweet.	Making this dangerous time extremely pleasant.
Exit	*EXIT*

58

Act 2 Scene 1

ORIGINAL TEXT	MODERN TRANSLATION
A lane by the wall of Capulet's orchard.	A lane by the wall of Capulet's orchard.
Enter ROMEO	*Enter ROMEO*
ROMEO Can I go forward when my heart is here? Turn back, dull earth, and find thy centre out. *He climbs the wall, and leaps down within it*	**ROMEO** Can I leave when my heart is here? I have to turn back to where my heart is. *He climbs the wall, and leaps down within it.*
Enter BENVOLIO and MERCUTIO	*Enter BENVOLIO and MERCUTIO*
BENVOLIO Romeo! my cousin Romeo!	**BENVOLIO** Romeo! Cousin Romeo!
MERCUTIO He is wise; And, on my lie, hath stol'n him home to bed.	**MERCUTIO** He's a clever lad; I bet he just went home to bed.
BENVOLIO He ran this way, and leap'd this orchard wall: Call, good Mercutio.	**BENVOLIO** He ran over here, and jumped over the orchard wall: Shout for him, Mercutio.
MERCUTIO Nay, I'll conjure too. Romeo! humours! madman! passion! lover! Appear thou in the likeness of a sigh: Speak but one rhyme, and I am satisfied; Cry but 'Ay me!' pronounce but 'love' and 'dove;' Speak to my gossip Venus one fair word, One nick-name for her purblind son and heir, Young Adam Cupid, he that shot so trim, When King Cophetua loved the beggar-maid! He heareth not, he stirreth not, he moveth not; The ape is dead, and I must conjure him. I conjure thee by Rosaline's bright eyes, By her high forehead and her scarlet lip, By her fine foot, straight leg and quivering thigh And the demesnes that there adjacent lie, That in thy likeness thou appear to us!	**MERCUTIO** No, I'll conjure him up like a spirit. Romeo! Madman! Passion! Lover! Appear as a sigh: Speak in rhyme just once, and I will be happy; Shout just 'ah me!' say just 'love' and 'dove;' Say just one nice thing to Venus, One mention of Cupid's nick-name. The one who shot arrows so well In the classic love story! He cannot hear, he's not interested; Silly Romeo is dead; I must conjure his spirit. I conjure you by Rosaline's beautiful eyes, By her foreheard and her lips, Her lovely feet, straight leg and shaking thighs And the area just next to her thigh, Appear to us!

BENVOLIO

And if he hear thee, thou wilt anger him.

MERCUTIO

This cannot anger him: 'twould anger him

To raise a spirit in his mistress' circle

Of some strange nature, letting it there stand
Till she had laid it and conjured it down;
That were some spite: my invocation
Is fair and honest, and in his mistres s' name

I conjure only but to raise up him.

BENVOLIO

Come, he hath hid himself among these trees,
To be consorted with the humorous night:
Blind is his love and best befits the dark.

MERCUTIO

If love be blind, love cannot hit the mark.
Now will he sit under a medlar tree,

And wish his mistress were that kind of fruit
As maids call medlars, when they laugh alone.
Romeo, that she were, O, that she were
An open et caetera, thou a poperin pear!
Romeo, good night: I'll to my truckle-bed;
This field-bed is too cold for me to sleep:
Come, shall we go?

BENVOLIO

Go, then; for 'tis in vain
To seek him here that means not to be found.

Exeunt

BENVOLIO

If he hears you, you're going to annoy him.

MERCUTIO

This won't annoy him: 'it would make him angry
To raise a spirit to have sex with his woman

That would annoy him: what I am doing
Is fair and honest, and I only mention Rosaline's name
To get his attention.

BENVOLIO:

Come on, he's hidden in the trees,
To be alone with the night:
His love is blind so it fits in best in the dark.

MERCUTIO

If love is blind, it cannot hit its target.
Now he'll sit under a tree which looks like a woman's genitalia
And wish his woman was like that fruit

Romeo, I wish she were one of those fruits
And you could pop into it!
Romeo, good night: I'm going to bed;
It's too cold for me to sleep out here:
Come on, shall we go?

BENVOLIO

Go, then, it's pointless
Looking for him here when he doesn't want to be found.

Exit

Act 2 Scene 2

ORIGINAL TEXT	MODERN TRANSLATION
Capulet's orchard.	Capulet's orchard.
Enter ROMEO	*Enter ROMEO*
ROMEO He jests at scars that never felt a wound.	**ROMEO** Mercutio winds me up about things that he's never experienced himself.
JULIET appears above at a window	*JULIET appears at a window*
But, soft! what light through yonder window breaks? It is the east, and Juliet is the sun. Arise, fair sun, and kill the envious moon, Who is already sick and pale with grief, That thou her maid art far more fair than she: Be not her maid, since she is envious;	But, shh! What light shines at that window? It is Juliet, like the sun rising from the east. Rise, sun, kill the jealous moon, Who is already sick and pale with sadness, That you are more beautiful than her: Don't be hers anymore, since she is jealous;
Her vestal livery is but sick and green And none but fools do wear it; cast it off.	She looks sick because she is still a virgin And only fools keep their virginity; get rid of it.
It is my lady, O, it is my love! O, that she knew she were! She speaks yet she says nothing: what of that?	It is my lady, oh, the one I love! I wish she knew I loved her! She is speaking but is not saying anything: what does that matter?
Her eye discourses; I will answer it. I am too bold, 'tis not to me she speaks:	Her eyes are speaking; I will answer. I am too cocky, it's not me she's speaking to:
Two of the fairest stars in all the heaven, Having some business, do entreat her eyes	Two of the prettiest stars in the sky, Had to go away on business, and asked her eyes
To twinkle in their spheres till they return.	To shine in their place until they come back.
What if her eyes were there, they in her head?	If her eyes were in the sky and the stars were in her face,
The brightness of her cheek would shame those stars, As daylight doth a lamp; her eyes in heaven	The stars would look dull compared to her shining cheeks, As the sun outshines a lamp; her eyes in the sky
Would through the airy region stream so bright That birds would sing and think it were not night.	Would be so bright That birds would sing in the night-time, thinking it was still day.
See, how she leans her cheek upon her hand!	See how she is leaning her cheek on her hand!

O, that I were a glove upon that hand,

That I might touch that cheek!

JULIET
Ay me!

ROMEO
She speaks:
O, speak again, bright angel! for thou art
As glorious to this night, being o'er my head
As is a winged messenger of heaven
Unto the white-upturned wondering eyes
Of mortals that fall back to gaze on him
When he bestrides the lazy-pacing clouds
And sails upon the bosom of the air.

JULIET
O Romeo, Romeo! wherefore art thou Romeo?

Deny thy father and refuse thy name;

Or, if thou wilt not, be but sworn my love,
And I'll no longer be a Capulet.

ROMEO
[Aside] Shall I hear more, or shall I speak at this?

JULIET
'Tis but thy name that is my enemy;

Thou art thyself, though not a Montague.

What's Montague? it is nor hand, nor foot,
Nor arm, nor face, nor any other part
Belonging to a man. O, be some other name!

What's in a name? that which we call a rose
By any other name would smell as sweet;

So Romeo would, were he not Romeo call'd,

Retain that dear perfection which he owes
Without that title. Romeo, doff thy name,

And for that name which is no part of thee

Take all myself.

Oh, I would love to be a glove on that hand.
So I could touch her cheek too!

JULIET
Oh my!

ROMEO
She speaks:
O, speak again, bright angel! For you are
As amazing
As an angel
That appears to
Humans who are awe-struck
When he walks along the sky
And flys around in the air.

JULIET
Oh Romeo, Romeo! Why do you have to be Romeo?
Abandon your family and your family name;
Or, if you won't, just tell me you love me,
And I will leave the Capulet family.

ROMEO
(quietly) Shall I carry on listening, or shall I say something?

JULIET
Only your family name of Montague is my enemy;
You'd still be you, if you weren't a Montague.
What is Montague? It's not hand or foot,
Or arm, face or any other bit
Of a man's body. Oh, be from another family!
What is important about a name? If a rose
Was called something else it would still smell just as great;
Romeo is the same - if he wasn't a Montague,
He'd still keep the perfection he now has
Without that surname. Romeo, abandon your name.
And to replace your name which is unimportant
Take all of me.

ROMEO
I take thee at thy word:
Call me but love, and I'll be new baptized;

Henceforth I never will be Romeo.

JULIET
What man art thou that thus bescreen'd in night
So stumblest on my counsel?

ROMEO
By a name
I know not how to tell thee who I am:
My name, dear saint, is hateful to myself,
Because it is an enemy to thee;
Had I it written, I would tear the word.

JULIET
My ears have not yet drunk a hundred words
Of that tongue's utterance, yet I know the sound:
Art thou not Romeo and a Montague?

ROMEO
Neither, fair saint, if either thee dislike.

JULIET
How camest thou hither, tell me, and wherefore?
The orchard walls are high and hard to climb,

And the place death, considering who thou art,

If any of my kinsmen find thee here.

ROMEO
With love's light wings did I o'er-perch these walls;
For stony limits cannot hold love out,
And what love can do that dares love attempt;

Therefore thy kinsmen are no let to me.

JULIET
If they do see thee, they will murder thee.

ROMEO
Alack, there lies more peril in thine eye

Than twenty of their swords: look thou but sweet,

And I am proof against their enmity.

ROMEO
I will trust what you are saying:
Call me your love, and I'll change my name;
From now on I won't be Romeo.

JULIET
Who are you, that listens to my private thoughts?

ROMEO
My name
I can't tell you who I am:
My name is something I myself hate,
Because it makes me your enemy;
If I had it written down, I would tear it up.

JULIET
I have heard only a few lines from you
yet I know who you are:
Aren't you Romeo of the Montague family?

ROMEO
I will be neither if you don't like it.

JULIET
How did you get here? Tell me, and why?
The orchard walls are high up and difficult to climb up.
And this place will be your death, when you think about who you are,
If any of my people find you here.

ROMEO
Love helped me fly over the walls;
Stony walls can't hold love out,
And love makes a man be able to do anything;
So your men don't worry me.

JULIET
If they see you they will kill you.

ROMEO
There is more danger in a bad look from you
Than twenty of their swords: if you look sweetly at me,
I will be invincible to their attacks.

JULIET

I would not for the world they saw thee here.

ROMEO

I have night's cloak to hide me from their sight;
And but thou love me, let them find me here:
My life were better ended by their hate,
Than death prorogued, wanting of thy love.

JULIET

By whose direction found'st thou out this place?

ROMEO

By love, who first did prompt me to inquire;

He lent me counsel and I lent him eyes.

I am no pilot; yet, wert thou as far

As that vast shore wash'd with the farthest sea,
I would adventure for such merchandise.

JULIET

Thou know'st the mask of night is on my face,
Else would a maiden blush bepaint my cheek
For that which thou hast heard me speak to-night
Fain would I dwell on form, fain, fain deny

What I have spoke: but farewell compliment!
Dost thou love me? I know thou wilt say 'Ay,'
And I will take thy word: yet if thou swear'st,
Thou mayst prove false; at lovers' perjuries
Then say, Jove laughs. O gentle Romeo,

If thou dost love, pronounce it faithfully:
Or if thou think'st I am too quickly won,

I'll frown and be perverse an say thee nay,
So thou wilt woo; but else, not for the world.
In truth, fair Montague, I am too fond,
And therefore thou mayst think my 'havior light:
But trust me, gentleman, I'll prove more true

Than those that have more cunning to be strange.

I should have been more strange, I must confess,
But that thou overheard'st, ere I was ware,
My true love's passion: therefore pardon me,
And not impute this yielding to light love,
Which the dark night hath so discovered.

JULIET

I really don't want them to see you here.

ROMEO

The darkness of night keeps me hidden:
And if you don't love me, let them find me:
I'd rather they killed me,
Than die slowly with you not loving me.

JULIET

Who showed you how to get here?

ROMEO

Love showed me; he made me want to come;
He gave me advice and showed me the way to go.
I am not a sailor; but even if you were as far away
As the further sea could take you,
I'd risk the journey to get to you.

JULIET

You know the dark of night hides my face,
Else you'd see that I am blushing
For what you heard me say earlier.
I would (for good manners)pretend I had not said
What I said: but forget manners!
Do you love me? I know you will say 'yes'
And I will believe you: if you promise,
You may prove to be lying; at lovers' lies,
They say the King of the gods laughs. Oh Romeo,
If you do love me, tell me honestly:
Or if you think I have fallen for you too easily,
I'll play hard to get,
So you will have to woo me; but otherwise
The truth is, I love you too much,
And so you may think I am too easily won:
But honestly, I will prove to be more faithful
Than girls who pretend one thing and act another.
I should have been more reserved, it's true
But I didn't know you were listening to me.
My true love is you; so forgive me.
And do not assume because I love you so easily, that my love isn't real.

ROMEO
Lady, by yonder blessed moon I swear
That tips with silver all these fruit-tree tops--

JULIET
O, swear not by the moon, the inconstant moon,

That monthly changes in her circled orb,
Lest that thy love prove likewise variable.

ROMEO
What shall I swear by?

JULIET
Do not swear at all;
Or, if thou wilt, swear by thy gracious self,
Which is the god of my idolatry,
And I'll believe thee.

ROMEO
If my heart's dear love--

JULIET
Well, do not swear: although I joy in thee,

I have no joy of this contract to-night:
It is too rash, too unadvised, too sudden;
Too like the lightning, which doth cease to be
Ere one can say 'It lightens.' Sweet, good night!

This bud of love, by summer's ripening breath,
May prove a beauteous flower when next we meet.

Good night, good night! as sweet repose and rest

Come to thy heart as that within my breast!

ROMEO
O, wilt thou leave me so unsatisfied?

JULIET
What satisfaction canst thou have to-night?

ROMEO
The exchange of thy love's faithful vow for mine.

JULIET
I gave thee mine before thou didst request it:
And yet I would it were to give again.

ROMEO
Lady, by the moon I promise
That covers the tree tops in silver light.

JULIET
Oh, don't promise by the moon, which
goes away,
Changes and moves in her orbit,
Let your love not be like that.

ROMEO
What shall I promise by?

JULIET
Don't promise at all:
Or if you will, promise by yourself,
Which is the thing I worship.
And I will believe you.

ROMEO
If my heart's dear love...

JULIET
Well, do not swear at all: although you
make me joyful,
A vow of love tonight will not:
It is too soon, too unprepared;
Too much like lightning, which disappears
As soon as a person sees it. Darling, good
night!
This tiny flower bud of love, with time
May grow into a beautiful flower when we
see each other again.
Good night, good night! Enjoy a rest as
peaceful and sweet
As the feelings within my heart!

ROMEO
Oh, will you leave me like this, unsatisfied?

JULIET
What satisfaction can you have tonight?

ROMEO
For you to tell me that you love me.

JULIET
I loved you before you even asked:
If I could take it back I would.

ROMEO
Wouldst thou withdraw it? for what purpose, love?

JULIET
But to be frank, and give it thee again.
And yet I wish but for the thing I have:
My bounty is as boundless as the sea,

My love as deep; the more I give to thee,

The more I have, for both are infinite.

Nurse calls within

I hear some noise within; dear love, adieu!
Anon, good nurse! Sweet Montague, be true.

Stay but a little, I will come again.

Exit, above

ROMEO
O blessed, blessed night! I am afeard.
Being in night, all this is but a dream,
Too flattering-sweet to be substantial.

Re-enter JULIET, above

JULIET
Three words, dear Romeo, and good night indeed.

If that thy bent of love be honourable,
Thy purpose marriage, send me word to-morrow,

By one that I'll procure to come to thee,
Where and what time thou wilt perform the rite;

And all my fortunes at thy foot I'll lay
And follow thee my lord throughout the world.

Nurse
[Within] Madam!

JULIET
I come, anon.--But if thou mean'st not well,
I do beseech thee--

Nurse
[Within] Madam!

ROMEO
You would take it back? Why?

JULIET
So I could give it to you again.
Yet I wish for the thing I have:
My generosity towards you is as huge as the sea,
My love is as deep; the more love I give you,
The more I have, for my love is never ending.

Nurse calls from within the house

I hear noise within the house: lover, goodbye!
Ok, nurse! Sweet Montague, be true.
Stay here a minute, I will come back.

Juliet exits above

ROMEO
O blessed night! I am afraid;
Because it is night, all this is just a dream.
It's too flattering to be real.

JULIET comes back, above

JULIET
Three words, Romeo, and I am going for real.
If your love for me is real,
And you want to marry me, send a message tomorrow,
By someone I will send to you,
Tell me the time and place our marriage will take place;
And I will give you everything I have
And follow you as my leader throughout the whole world.

Nurse
(inside) Madam!

JULIET
I am coming...but if you mean to trick me,
I beg you...

Nurse
(within) Madam!

JULIET
By and by, I come:--
To cease thy suit, and leave me to my grief:

To-morrow will I send.

ROMEO
So thrive my soul--

JULIET
A thousand times good night!

Exit, above

ROMEO
A thousand times the worse, to want thy light.

Love goes toward love, as schoolboys from
their books,
But love from love, toward school with heavy looks.

Retiring

Re-enter JULIET, above

JULIET
Hist! Romeo, hist! O, for a falconer's voice,

To lure this tassel-gentle back again!
Bondage is hoarse, and may not speak aloud;
Else would I tear the cave where Echo lies,

And make her airy tongue more hoarse than mine,
With repetition of my Romeo's name.

ROMEO
It is my soul that calls upon my name:

How silver-sweet sound lovers' tongues by night,
Like softest music to attending ears!

JULIET
Romeo!

ROMEO
My dear?

JULIET
At what o'clock to-morrow

JULIET
I am coming...
Stop your pursuit of me, and leave me to
be upset:
Tomorrow I will send someone.

ROMEO
My soul depends on it...

JULIET
A thousand times good night!

Exit, above

ROMEO
It's a thousands times worse to be without
you than with you.
Going to one you love, is like school kids
running away from their school work,
But leaving the one you love, is as hard as
going back to school.

Going away

Re-enter JULIET above

JULIET
Psst! Romeo, psst! Oh, for a special
whistle,
To bring my bird back again!
I'm trapped here so cannot be loud;
Otherwise I would shout my head off,
And the echo would sound for ages,
Its voice would get warn out,
Repeating Romeo's name.

ROMEO
My name is being called - it is my soul that
does it:
The sound of lovers' voices is so sweet,
Like the softest music in my ears!

JULIET
Romeo!

ROMEO
My love?

JULIET
What time tomorrow

Shall I send to thee?

ROMEO
At the hour of nine.

JULIET
I will not fail: 'tis twenty years till then.
I have forgot why I did call thee back.

ROMEO
Let me stand here till thou remember it.

JULIET
I shall forget, to have thee still stand there,

Remembering how I love thy company.

ROMEO
And I'll still stay, to have thee still forget,
Forgetting any other home but this.

JULIET
'Tis almost morning; I would have thee gone:
And yet no further than a wanton's bird;
Who lets it hop a little from her hand,
Like a poor prisoner in his twisted gyves,
And with a silk thread plucks it back again,
So loving-jealous of his liberty.

ROMEO
I would I were thy bird.

JULIET
Sweet, so would I:
Yet I should kill thee with much cherishing.

Good night, good night! parting is such
sweet sorrow,
That I shall say good night till it be morrow.

Exit above

ROMEO
Sleep dwell upon thine eyes, peace in thy breast!
Would I were sleep and peace, so sweet to rest!

Hence will I to my ghostly father's cell,
His help to crave, and my dear hap to tell.

Exit

Shall I send someone to you?

ROMEO
At nine o clock.

JULIET
I will do it, although it feels years away.
I forget why I called you back.

ROMEO
I will wait here until you remember.

JULIET
I will forget on purpose, so you stand
there,
I love spending time with you.

ROMEO
And I will stay here,
Forgetting everything but this moment.

JULIET
It's almost morning; I want you to go:
But not too far away, like a pet bird;
So I can let you hop a little distance,
Like a prisoner in chains,
And then pull you back again,
Jealous of your freedom.

ROMEO
I wish I was your bird.

JULIET
So do I:
But I would kill you with much love, by
squashing you.
Good night, good night! Going away is so
sad,
I shall say goodbye but see you tomorrow.

Exit

ROMEO
Sleep come to you, heart be at peace!
I wish I was sleep and peace, so I could lie
on you!
I will go to the priest
asking for his help.

Exit

Act 2 Scene 3

ORIGINAL TEXT	MODERN TRANSLATION
Friar Laurence's cell.	Friar Laurence's room.
Enter FRIAR LAURENCE, with a basket	*Enter FRIAR LAURENCE, carrying a basket*
FRIAR LAURENCE The grey-eyed morn smiles on the frowning night,	**FRIAR LAURENCE** The happy morning is arriving and replacing the frowning night,
Chequering the eastern clouds with streaks of light, And flecked darkness like a drunkard reels From forth day's path and Titan's fiery wheels: Now, ere the sun advance his burning eye, The day to cheer and night's dank dew to dry, I must up-fill this osier cage of ours With baleful weeds and precious-juiced flowers.	The darkness is streaked with sunlight, And darkness stumbles away From the sunlight Now, before the sun rises fully, And dries up the wetness on the ground, I must fill up this basket With poisonous weeds and medicinal flowers.
The earth that's nature's mother is her tomb; What is her burying grave that is her womb, And from her womb children of divers kind We sucking on her natural bosom find, Many for many virtues excellent, None but for some and yet all different. O, mickle is the powerful grace that lies In herbs, plants, stones, and their true qualities: For nought so vile that on the earth doth live But to the earth some special good doth give, Nor aught so good but strain'd from that fair use Revolts from true birth, stumbling on abuse: Virtue itself turns vice, being misapplied; And vice sometimes by action dignified. Within the infant rind of this small flower Poison hath residence and medicine power: For this, being smelt, with that part cheers each part; Being tasted, slays all senses with the heart. Two such opposed kings encamp them still In man as well as herbs, grace and rude will; And where the worser is predominant, Full soon the canker death eats up that plant.	The earth, where nature lives and dies; Both buries and gives birth to her, And from the womb of nature We find lots of nourishment, Many things for good purposes, Some are for very bad purposes. Oh, there is great power In herbs and plants: For there is nothing alive on earth That cannot be used for good, Or anything that can also be used for bad Misused, good things turn bad, and bad things turn good. Inside this tiny flower Poison lives, but also powerful medicine: If you smell it, it makes you feel better; If you eat it, it kills you. Two opposing forces live together In humans as well as in plants; And where the evil is strongest, Death will win.
Enter ROMEO	*Enter ROMEO*
ROMEO Good morrow, father.	**ROMEO** Good morning, father.
FRIAR LAURENCE Benedicite!	**FRIAR LAURENCE** God bless you!

What early tongue so sweet saluteth me?	Who welcomes me so early in the morning?
Young son, it argues a distemper'd head So soon to bid good morrow to thy bed: Care keeps his watch in every old man's eye, And where care lodges, sleep will never lie; But where unbruised youth with unstuff'd brain Doth couch his limbs, there golden sleep doth reign: Therefore thy earliness doth me assure	Young son, it suggests you are in trouble To get up so early out of your bed: All old men have their own troubles, And therefore do not sleep much; But when a young, care-free youth Does go to bed, there he sleeps peacefully: Therefore the fact that you are up so early tells me
Thou art up-roused by some distemperature; Or if not so, then here I hit it right,	You are in some sort of trouble; Or if that is not the case then how about this,
Our Romeo hath not been in bed to-night.	You haven't even gone to bed tonight.

ROMEO

That last is true; the sweeter rest was mine.	That last bit was right, although I still had sweet rest.

FRIAR LAURENCE

God pardon sin! wast thou with Rosaline?	God forgive you! Have you spent the night with Rosaline?

ROMEO

With Rosaline, my ghostly father? no; I have forgot that name, and that name's woe.	With Rosaline, my shocked priest? no; I have forgotten her and everything about her.

FRIAR LAURENCE

That's my good son: but where hast thou been, then?	That's good; but where have you been then?

ROMEO

I'll tell thee, ere thou ask it me again. I have been feasting with mine enemy, Where on a sudden one hath wounded me, That's by me wounded: both our remedies Within thy help and holy physic lies: I bear no hatred, blessed man, for, lo, My intercession likewise steads my foe.	I'll tell you, before you ask me again. I have been eating with my enemy, Where one of them wounded me, And I wounded them: to heal both of us Your help is needed: I have no hate, blessed man, because, My request will help my enemy too.

FRIAR LAURENCE

Be plain, good son, and homely in thy drift; Riddling confession finds but riddling shrift.	Speak plainly, son, and quickly tell me; Speaking in riddles does no-one any good.

ROMEO

Then plainly know my heart's dear love is set On the fair daughter of rich Capulet: As mine on hers, so hers is set on mine; And all combined, save what thou must combine	The plain truth is that I am in love With the daughter of Lord Capulet: I love her and she loves me; And altogether, save us

By holy marriage: when and where and how
We met, we woo'd and made exchange of vow,
I'll tell thee as we pass; but this I pray,
That thou consent to marry us to-day.

FRIAR LAURENCE
Holy Saint Francis, what a change is here!
Is Rosaline, whom thou didst love so dear,
So soon forsaken? young men's love then lies

Not truly in their hearts, but in their eyes.
Jesu Maria, what a deal of brine
Hath wash'd thy sallow cheeks for Rosaline!
How much salt water thrown away in waste,
To season love, that of it doth not taste!
The sun not yet thy sighs from heaven clears,
Thy old groans ring yet in my ancient ears;

Lo, here upon thy cheek the stain doth sit
Of an old tear that is not wash'd off yet:
If e'er thou wast thyself and these woes thine,

Thou and these woes were all for Rosaline:
And art thou changed? pronounce this sentence then,
Women may fall, when there's no strength in men.

ROMEO
Thou chid'st me oft for loving Rosaline.

FRIAR LAURENCE
For doting, not for loving, pupil mine.

ROMEO
And bad'st me bury love.

FRIAR LAURENCE
Not in a grave,
To lay one in, another out to have.

ROMEO
I pray thee, chide not; she whom I love now

Doth grace for grace and love for love allow;
The other did not so.

FRIAR LAURENCE
O, she knew well
Thy love did read by rote and could not spell.

By marrying us; when and where and how
We met, flirted and fell in love,
I'll tell you in a bit, but this please do,
Promise you will marry us today.

FRIAR LAURENCE
Holy Saint Francis, here is a huge change!
Is Rosaline, who you did love so much,
So quickly forgotten? Young men's love then lives
Not in their hearts but in their eyes.
Jesus and Mary, how many tears
Did you cry for Rosaline?
How many salty tears were shed in waste,
To season a love which you never did eat!
The sun hasn't yet burnt up all your sighs,
Your previous groaning still rings in my ears;
And her on your cheek there is still a stain
Of a tear cried for Rosaline:
If ever you were yourself and these sadnesses yours,
They were sadnesses just for Rosaline:
Have you changed? Repeat after me then:

Women can't be expected to be faithful, when men are so weak.

ROMEO
You were always telling me off for loving Rosaline.

FRIAR LAURENCE
For obsessing about her, not loving her.

ROMEO
And you told me to get kill off my love.

FRIAR LAURENCE
Not to bury it,
And to replace it with another one.

ROMEO
I beg you, don't tell me off, she who I now love
Loves me too;
Rosaline did not.

FRIAR LAURENCE
Oh, she knew very well
Your love was not real.

But come, young waverer, come, go with me, In one respect I'll thy assistant be; For this alliance may so happy prove, To turn your households' rancour to pure love.	But come on, come with me, I will help you; For this marriage may be a good thing, To turn the two enemy families to friendship.
ROMEO O, let us hence; I stand on sudden haste.	**ROMEO** Oh hurry up then; I need to hurry.
FRIAR LAURENCE Wisely and slow; they stumble that run fast.	**FRIAR LAURENCE** Slow down, those who run fast trip over.
Exeunt	*Exit*

ORIGINAL TEXT	MODERN TRANSLATION
A street.	A street
Enter BENVOLIO and MERCUTIO	*Enter BENVOLIO and MERCUTIO*
MERCUTIO Where the devil should this Romeo be? Came he not home to-night?	**MERCUTIO** Where is Romeo? Did he not come home tonight?
BENVOLIO Not to his father's; I spoke with his man.	**BENVOLIO** Not to his dad's house; I spoke with one of the men there.
MERCUTIO Ah, that same pale hard-hearted wench, that Rosaline. Torments him so, that he will sure run mad.	**MERCUTIO** Ah, that tough woman Rosaline. Upsets him so much, he will become mad.
BENVOLIO Tybalt, the kinsman of old Capulet, Hath sent a letter to his father's house.	**BENVOLIO** Tybalt, the relative of Lord Capulet. Has sent a letter to Romeo's dad's house.
MERCUTIO A challenge, on my life.	**MERCUTIO** A challenge to fight, I bet.
BENVOLIO Romeo will answer it.	**BENVOLIO** Romeo will answer it.
MERCUTIO Any man that can write may answer a letter.	**MERCUTIO** Any man who can write can answer a letter.
BENVOLIO Nay, he will answer the letter's master, how he dares, being dared.	**BENVOLIO** No, he will answer Tybalt by fighting him.
MERCUTIO Alas poor Romeo! he is already dead; stabbed with a white wench's black eye; shot through the ear with a love-song; the very pin of his heart cleft with the blind bow-boy's butt-shaft: and is he a man to encounter Tybalt?	**MERCUTIO** Ah, poor Romeo! He is already dead; Stabbed with a woman's eye; shot through the ear with a love song; his heart broken by an arrow from Cupid's bow. And is he brave enough to fight Tybalt?
BENVOLIO Why, what is Tybalt?	**BENVOLIO** Why, what's so special about Tybalt?
MERCUTIO More than prince of cats, I can tell you. O, he is	**MERCUTIO** More than the legend from who he takes his name, I can tell you

the courageous captain of compliments. He fights as you sing prick-song, keeps time, distance, and proportion; rests me his minim rest, one, two, and the third in your bosom: the very butcher of a silk button, a duellist, a duellist; a gentleman of the very first house, of the first and second cause: ah, the immortal passado! the punto reverso! the hai!

He is courageous. He fights very well
Like a dance.
He rests one, two and at the third one you are stabbed in the heart. He is a fighter, a student of the
best school of duelling, he knows
the forward thrust! The backward thrust!
And the thrust which goes right through you!

BENVOLIO
The what?

BENVOLIO
The what?

MERCUTIO
The pox of such antic, lisping, affecting fantasticoes; these new tuners of accents! 'By Jesu,

a very good blade! a very tall man! a very good

whore!' Why, is not this a lamentable thing, grandsire, that we should be thus afflicted with these strange flies, these fashion-mongers, these perdona-mi's, who stand so much on the new form, that they cannot at ease on the old bench? O, their bones, their bones!

MERCUTIO
I hate these silly men who talk in the latest fashionable ways and with silly accents! 'By Jesus,
a very good blade! a very tall man! a very good
whore!' Isn't it sad,
that people speak in such stupid ways,
to be fashionable,
they copy the latest fashions,
sitting back on an old bench they cry O, their aching bones.

Enter ROMEO

Enter ROMEO

BENVOLIO
Here comes Romeo, here comes Romeo.

BENVOLIO
Here comes Romeo, here comes Romeo.

MERCUTIO
Without his roe, like a dried herring: flesh, flesh, how art thou fishified! Now is he for the numbers that Petrarch flowed in: Laura to his lady was but a kitchen-wench; marry, she had a better love to be-rhyme her; Dido a dowdy; Cleopatra a gipsy; Helen and Hero hildings and harlots; Thisbe a grey eye or so, but not to the purpose. Signior Romeo, bon jour! there's a French salutation to your French slop. You gave us the counterfeit fairly last night.

MERCUTIO
Like a dried fish, without his eggs,
Now he's ready for Petrarch's love poetry:
Laura (who Petrarch loved) when compared to his lady was just a kitchen slave. Admittedly, she had a better love to write poems for her; Dido was a rubbish dresser; Cleopatra a gypsy; Helen and Hero were sluts and prostitutes; Thisbe might have had a blue eye or two, but it doesn't matter. Mister Romeo, hello! There's a French hello to your French outfit. You cheated us last night.

ROMEO
Good morrow to you both. What counterfeit did I give you?

ROMEO
Good morning to both of you. How did I cheat you?

MERCUTIO
The ship, sir, the slip; can you not conceive?

MERCUTIO
You disappeared, don't you remember?

ROMEO
Pardon, good Mercutio, my business was great; and in
such a case as mine a man may strain courtesy.

ROMEO
Sorry, Mercutio, I had something important to do; and in
such a situation like mine it is OK to forget politeness.

MERCUTIO
That's as much as to say, such a case as yours constrains a man to bow in the hams.

MERCUTIO
You're saying that important business was to go and have sex, shaking your buttocks.

ROMEO
Meaning, to court'sy.

ROMEO
Shaking my buttocks by doing a curtsey.

MERCUTIO
Thou hast most kindly hit it.

MERCUTIO
You got it right.

ROMEO
A most courteous exposition.

ROMEO
What a polite explanation.

MERCUTIO
Nay, I am the very pink of courtesy.

MERCUTIO
I am the pink flower of politeness.

ROMEO
Pink for flower.

ROMEO
Pink flower as in a woman's genitalia.

MERCUTIO
Right.

MERCUTIO
Right.

ROMEO
Why, then is my pump well flowered.

ROMEO
Well then my penis has seen many pink flowers.

MERCUTIO
Well said: follow me this jest now till thou hast worn out thy pump, that when the single sole of it is worn, the jest may remain after the wearing sole singular.

MERCUTIO
Well said: this joke has

worn you out, when the joke is over
You have nothing left.

ROMEO
O single-soled jest, solely singular for the singleness.

ROMEO
Oh what a bad joke; this is all just stupidity.

MERCUTIO
Come between us, good Benvolio; my wits faint.

MERCUTIO
Come and break this up, Benvolio, I am losing this battle.

ROMEO
Switch and spurs, switch and spurs; or I'll cry a match.

ROMEO
Carry on, else I shall declare myself the winner.

MERCUTIO
Nay, if thy wits run the wild-goose chase, I have done, for thou hast more of the wild-goose in one of thy wits than, I am sure, I have in my whole five: was I with you there for the goose?

ROMEO
Thou wast never with me for any thing when thou wast
not there for the goose.

MERCUTIO
I will bite thee by the ear for that jest.

ROMEO
Nay, good goose, bite not.

MERCUTIO
Thy wit is a very bitter sweeting; it is a most sharp sauce.

ROMEO
And is it not well served in to a sweet goose?

MERCUTIO
O here's a wit of cheveril, that stretches from an inch narrow to an ell broad!

ROMEO
I stretch it out for that word 'broad;' which added to the goose, proves thee far and wide a broad goose.

MERCUTIO
Why, is not this better now than groaning for love?

now art thou sociable, now art thou Romeo; now art thou what thou art, by art as well as by nature: for this drivelling love is like a great natural, that runs lolling up and down to hide his bauble in a hole.

BENVOLIO
Stop there, stop there.

MERCUTIO
Thou desirest me to stop in my tale against the hair.

MERCUTIO
No, if this carries on,
I am done for
You have more humour than me.
Was I even close to being equal to you?

ROMEO
You were never with me.

MERCUTIO
I'll get you for that joke.

ROMEO
No, please don't bite me goose.

MERCUTIO
Your humour is hurtful; it's hard to take.

ROMEO
It's a good sauce to serve with a sweet goose like you.

MERCUTIO
Oh now you're stretching the joke too far and too thin!

ROMEO
I will stretch it out further, goose.

MERCUTIO
Now, isn't this banter much better than being upset and depressed in love?
You are now fun to be around Romeo;
You are now what nature made you to be:
For this depressing love is like an idiot,
Who runs up and down a hill looking to hide his toy in a hole.

BENVOLIO
Stop there, stop there.

MERCUTIO
You want me to stop in my story before it's finished.

BENVOLIO
Thou wouldst else have made thy tale large.

MERCUTIO
O, thou art deceived; I would have made it short:

for I was come to the whole depth of my tale; and meant, indeed, to occupy the argument no longer.

ROMEO
Here's goodly gear!

Enter Nurse and PETER

MERCUTIO
A sail, a sail!

BENVOLIO
Two, two; a shirt and a smock.

Nurse
Peter!

PETER
Anon!

Nurse
My fan, Peter.

MERCUTIO
Good Peter, to hide her face; for her fan's the fairer face.

Nurse
God ye good morrow, gentlemen.

MERCUTIO
God ye good den, fair gentlewoman.

Nurse
Is it good den?

MERCUTIO
'Tis no less, I tell you, for the bawdy hand of the dial is now upon the prick of noon.

Nurse
Out upon you! what a man are you!

BENVOLIO
Else it would be too long.

MERCUTIO
O you are wrong; I would have made it short:
For I had already told the whole story; and meant to say no more.

ROMEO
Here's something good.

Enter Nurse and PETER

MERCUTIO
Here comes a ship! A ship!

BENVOLIO
Two of them, a man and a woman.

Nurse
Peter!

Peter
I am here!

Nurse
Give me my fan, Peter.

MERCUTIO
Good Peter, the fan is to hide her face as the fan looks nicer.

Nurse
Good morning men.

MERCUTIO
Good afternoon, lady.

Nurse
Is it afternoon?

MERCUTIO
It is now, for the aroused hand of the clock is erect at noon. *(a sexual joke).*

Nurse
Get out of it! What kind of man are you!

ROMEO

One, gentlewoman, that God hath made for himself
tomar.

Nurse

By my troth, it is well said; 'for himself to mar,'
quoth a'? Gentlemen, can any of you tell me where I
may find the young Romeo?

ROMEO

I can tell you; but young Romeo will be older when

you have found him than he was when you sought
him:
I am the youngest of that name, for fault of a worse.

Nurse

You say well.

MERCUTIO

Yea, is the worst well? very well took, i' faith;
wisely, wisely.

Nurse

if you be he, sir, I desire some confidence with
you.

BENVOLIO

She will indite him to some supper.

MERCUTIO

A bawd, a bawd, a bawd! so ho!

ROMEO

What hast thou found?

MERCUTIO

No hare, sir; unless a hare, sir, in a lenten pie,
that is something stale and hoar ere it be spent.

Sings

An old hare hoar,
And an old hare hoar,
Is very good meat in lent
But a hare that is hoar
Is too much for a score,
When it hoars ere it be spent.
Romeo, will you come to your father's? we'll
to dinner, thither.

ROMEO

One, lady, that God has made for himself
to ruin.

Nurse

You are telling the truth; 'for himself to
ruin' Men, can any of you tell me
where I can find young Romeo?

ROMEO

I can tell you, but young Romeo will be
older
When you have found him than when he
was looked for:
I am Romeo, for better or worse.

Nurse

You speak well.

MERCUTIO

Is the worst well?

Nurse

If you are him, I would like to speak to you
alone.

BENVOLIO

She will invite him to a meal.

MERCUTIO

A pimp! a pimp! I've worked it out.

ROMEO

What have you worked out?

MERCUTIO

She's not a prostitute - she's too ugly.

sings

Old rabbit meat,
Old rabbit meat,
Is good to eat if it's all you can get,
But old rabbit meat,
Is no good,
When it rots before you eat it.
Romeo, will you come to your dad's? We'll
eat dinner there.

ROMEO
I will follow you.

MERCUTIO
Farewell, ancient lady; farewell,

Singing

'lady, lady, lady.'

Exeunt MERCUTIO and BENVOLIO

Nurse
Marry, farewell! I pray you, sir, what saucy
merchant was this, that was so full of his ropery?

ROMEO
A gentleman, nurse, that loves to hear himself talk,

and will speak more in a minute than he will stand

to in a month.

Nurse
An a' speak any thing against me, I'll take him

down, an a' were lustier than he is, and twenty such

Jacks; and if I cannot, I'll find those that shall.

Scurvy knave! I am none of his flirt-gills; I am
none of his skains-mates. And thou must stand by
too, and suffer every knave to use me at his
pleasure?

PETER
I saw no man use you a pleasure; if I had, my
weapon
should quickly have been out, I warrant you: I dare
draw as soon as another man, if I see occasion in a

good quarrel, and the law on my side.

Nurse
Now, afore God, I am so vexed, that every part
about
me quivers. Scurvy knave! Pray you, sir, a word:
and as I told you, my young lady bade me inquire
you
out; what she bade me say, I will keep to myself:

ROMEO
I will come after you.

MERCUTIO
Bye old lady, bye.

Singing

'lady, lady, lady.'

Exit MERCUTIO and BENVOLIO

Nurse
Goodbye! Please tell me, which rude
man was this, so full of himself?

ROMEO
A man, nurse, that loves to listen to
himself talk,
and will say more in a minute than he
actually does
in a whole month.

Nurse
If he says anything bad about me, I'll take
him
down, even if he were stronger than he is,
and had twenty men with him
If I cannot take him down, I'll find people
who can.
Dirty animal! I am not one of his hussies; I
am not one of his mates. And you just
stand there and let them be rude to me?

PETER
I didn't see anyone be rude to you; if I had,
my sword
would have been quickly out, I promise: I
shall pull my sword out, if I see the
opportunity
for a fight with the law on my side.

Nurse
Now, I promise, I am so stressed that
I am shaking.
Dirty animal! Please, sir, a word with you:
As I told you, my young lady asked me
to find you and the message I am to give
you I shall keep secret:

but first let me tell ye, if ye should lead her into

a fool's paradise, as they say, it were a very gross kind of behavior, as they say: for the gentlewoman is young; and, therefore, if you should deal double with her, truly it were an ill thing to be offered to any gentlewoman, and very weak dealing.

ROMEO
Nurse, commend me to thy lady and mistress. I protest unto thee--

Nurse
Good heart, and, i' faith, I will tell her as much: Lord, Lord, she will be a joyful woman.

ROMEO
What wilt thou tell her, nurse? thou dost not mark me.

Nurse
I will tell her, sir, that you do protest; which, as I take it, is a gentlemanlike offer.

ROMEO
Bid her devise
Some means to come to shrift this afternoon;
And there she shall at Friar Laurence' cell
Be shrived and married. Here is for thy pains.

Nurse
No truly sir; not a penny.

ROMEO
Go to; I say you shall.

Nurse
This afternoon, sir? well, she shall be there.

ROMEO
And stay, good nurse, behind the abbey wall:

Within this hour my man shall be with thee

And bring thee cords made like a tackled stair;
Which to the high top-gallant of my joy
Must be my convoy in the secret night.
Farewell; be trusty, and I'll quit thy pains:
Farewell; commend me to thy mistress.

But first let me say, if you are winding her up
Making promises you won't keep, it is a very bad thing to do,
the lady is young, and therefore if you are trying to trick her it would be very bad of you.

ROMEO
Nurse, speak well of me to Juliet.
I promise you…

NURSE
OK I will tell her:
She is a very happy girl.

ROMEO
What will you tell her? You do not listen to me.

Nurse
I will tell her, that you do protest to her *(the nurse means to use the word 'propose' here)*. It is an honourable offer.

ROMEO
Ask her to make up
Some reason to confession this afternoon;
And there, at Friar Laurence's,
She shall be married. Here's some money for your efforts.

Nurse
No, honestly I don't want a penny.

ROMEO
Go on, I say you shall have it.

Nurse
This afternoon? She shall be there.

ROMEO
And you stay behind the church wall
Nurse:
Within an hour my friend shall come to you
With a rope ladder;
Which I can climb up to Juliet
With at night.
Goodbye, be honest and I will repay you:
Goodbye, speak well of me to Juliet.

Nurse
Now God in heaven bless thee! Hark you, sir.

ROMEO
What say'st thou, my dear nurse?

Nurse
Is your man secret? Did you ne'er hear say,
Two may keep counsel, putting one away?

ROMEO
I warrant thee, my man's as true as steel.

NURSE
Well, sir; my mistress is the sweetest lady--Lord,
Lord! when 'twas a little prating thing:--O, there
is a nobleman in town, one Paris, that would fain
lay knife aboard; but she, good soul, had as lief
see a toad, a very toad, as see him. I anger her

sometimes and tell her that Paris is the properer
man; but, I'll warrant you, when I say so, she looks
as pale as any clout in the versal world. Doth not
rosemary and Romeo begin both with a letter?

ROMEO
Ay, nurse; what of that? both with an R.

Nurse
Ah. mocker! that's the dog's name; R is for
the--No; I know it begins with some other
letter:--and she hath the prettiest sententious of
it, of you and rosemary, that it would do you good
to hear it.

ROMEO
Commend me to thy lady.

Nurse
Ay, a thousand times.

Exit Romeo

Peter!

Nurse
Now, God bless you! Listen, sir.

ROMEO
What do you want to say?

Nurse
Can your friend keep a secret? Did you
never hear it said, two can plan the ruin of
one?

ROMEO
I promise, he's trustworthy.

NURSE
Well, sir, Juliet is the sweetest girl,
Oh, when she was a baby...Oh there
is a man in town, Paris, that would like
to marry her. But she doesn't want to
marry him. She would rather look at a toad
than him. I make her angry
Sometimes by saying that Paris is better
looking than you, but when I say it she
goes so pale. Doesn't Rosemary (a symbol
of remembrance for the dead and for
loved ones) and Romeo begin with the
same letter.

ROMEO
Yes, but what of it? They both begin with
the letter 'R'.

Nurse
Ah, joker! That's the dog's name. R is for
the...No, I know it's some other letter...
and she says the nicest things about you
You would love to hear it.

ROMEO
Speak well of me to Juliet.

Nurse
Yes, a thousand time.

Exit Romeo

Peter!

PETER Anon! **Nurse** Peter, take my fan, and go before and apace. *Exeunt*	**PETER** I am ready! **Nurse** Take my fan and walk before me. *Exit*

PETER
Anon!

Nurse
Peter, take my fan, and go before and apace.

82

ORIGINAL TEXT	MODERN TRANSLATION
Capulet's orchard.	Capulet's orchard.
Enter JULIET	*Enter Juliet*
JULIET	**JULIET**
The clock struck nine when I did send the nurse;	It was nine o'clock when I sent the nurse;
In half an hour she promised to return.	She said she'd be back within half an hour.
Perchance she cannot meet him: that's not so.	Maybe she did not meet him:
	that's not true.
O, she is lame! love's heralds should be thoughts,	Oh, she is slow! Love's messengers should
	be like thoughts,
Which ten times faster glide than the sun's beams,	Ten times faster than the speed of light,
Driving back shadows over louring hills:	Pushing back shadows over dark hills:
Therefore do nimble-pinion'd doves draw love,	That's how love should travel,
And therefore hath the wind-swift Cupid wings.	And that's why Cupid has wings to fly.
Now is the sun upon the highmost hill	Now it's midday
Of this day's journey, and from nine till twelve	And from nine till twelve
Is three long hours, yet she is not come.	Is three whole hours, yet she isn't here.
Had she affections and warm youthful blood,	If she was young and in love,
She would be as swift in motion as a ball;	She would be super quick;
My words would bandy her to my sweet love,	My words would bounce her to Romeo,
And his to me:	And his words bounce her back to me:
But old folks, many feign as they were dead;	But old people, many act like they are dead;
Unwieldy, slow, heavy and pale as lead.	Slow, laborious, heavy and pale.
O God, she comes!	Oh God, here she comes!
Enter Nurse and PETER	*Enter Nurse and PETER*
O honey nurse, what news?	Oh lovely nurse, what news do you have?
Hast thou met with him? Send thy man away.	Have you met him? Send Peter away.
Nurse	**Nurse**
Peter, stay at the gate.	Peter, wait at the gate.
Exit PETER	*Exit Peter*
JULIET	**JULIET**
Now, good sweet nurse,--O Lord, why look'st thou sad?	Sweet nurse...why do you look sad?
Though news be sad, yet tell them merrily;	Even if your news is sad, tell me with a smile;
If good, thou shamest the music of sweet news	If the news is good, you ruin it
By playing it to me with so sour a face.	with a sad face like that.

Nurse

I am a-weary, give me leave awhile:

Fie, how my bones ache! what a jaunt have I had!

JULIET

I would thou hadst my bones, and I thy news:

Nay, come, I pray thee, speak; good, good nurse, speak.

Nurse

Jesu, what haste? can you not stay awhile?

Do you not see that I am out of breath?

JULIET

How art thou out of breath, when thou hast breath

To say to me that thou art out of breath?
The excuse that thou dost make in this delay
Is longer than the tale thou dost excuse.

Is thy news good, or bad? answer to that;
Say either, and I'll stay the circumstance:

Let me be satisfied, is't good or bad?

Nurse

Well, you have made a simple choice; you know not how to choose a man: Romeo! no, not he; though his
face be better than any man's, yet his leg excels
all men's; and for a hand, and a foot, and a body,
though they be not to be talked on, yet they are
past compare: he is not the flower of courtesy,
but, I'll warrant him, as gentle as a lamb. Go thy
ways, wench; serve God. What, have you dined at
home?

JULIET

No, no: but all this did I know before.

What says he of our marriage? what of that?

Nurse

Lord, how my head aches! what a head have I!

It beats as it would fall in twenty pieces.

My back o' t' other side,--O, my back, my back!

Nurse

I am tired, give me a minute:
Oh, my bones ache! What a walk I've had!

JULIET

I wish you had my bones, and I had your news:
Come on, tell me, good good nurse. Tell me.

Nurse

Jesus, what a hurry? Can you not wait a minute?
Can't you see that I am out of breath?

JULIET

How can you be out of breath, when you have breath
to tell me you are out of breath?
Your excuse that you make in this delay
Takes longer to make than the message itself.
Is your news good or bad? Tell me that;
Say either one and I will wait for the details:
Satisfy me, is it good or bad?

Nurse

You've made a silly choice; you don't know how to choose a man: Romoe! No, not he;

though he is good looking,

He is not very polite.
But he is gentle. Do what you like.
Have you had lunch?

JULIET

No. Everything you just said I already knew.
What did he say about getting married?

Nurse

Oh my head hurts! What a headache I have!
It batters my head so bad I think it will fall into piece.
My back, on the other side, oh my back, my back!

Beshrew your heart for sending me about,
To catch my death with jaunting up and down!

JULIET
I' faith, I am sorry that thou art not well.
Sweet, sweet, sweet nurse, tell me, what says my love?

Nurse
Your love says, like an honest gentleman, and a courteous, and a kind, and a handsome, and, I warrant, a virtuous,--Where is your mother?

JULIET
Where is my mother! why, she is within;
Where should she be? How oddly thou repliest!

'Your love says, like an honest gentleman,
Where is your mother?'

Nurse
O God's lady dear!
Are you so hot? marry, come up, I trow;
Is this the poultice for my aching bones?

Henceforward do your messages yourself.

JULIET
Here's such a coil! come, what says Romeo?

Nurse
Have you got leave to go to shrift to-day?

JULIET
I have.

Nurse
Then hie you hence to Friar Laurence' cell;
There stays a husband to make you a wife:
Now comes the wanton blood up in your cheeks,
They'll be in scarlet straight at any news.
Hie you to church; I must another way,

To fetch a ladder, by the which your love
Must climb a bird's nest soon when it is dark:
I am the drudge and toil in your delight,
But you shall bear the burden soon at night.
Go; I'll to dinner: hie you to the cell.

Shame on you for sending me out,
To become so unwell whilst traipsing around.

JULIET
Honestly, I am sorry you are not well.
Sweet, sweet, sweet nurse, tell me, what did Romeo say?

Nurse
He says, like an honest man,
polite, kind, good look and
good...where is your mum?

JULIET
Where is my mum? She is indoors;
Where should she be? How stupid your reply!
'Your love says like an honest man where is your mum'?

Nurse
Oh Mary mother of Jesus!
Are you so impatient? Come on,
Is this going to make my aching bones better?
From now on take your own messages.

JULIET
You're moaning too much. What did Romeo say?

Nurse
Do you have permission to go to confession today?

JULIET
Yes.

Nurse
The go to Friar Laurence's place;
There is a husband to make you a wife:
Now the blood rushes to your cheeks,
Any news makes you blush.
Go to church; I have somewhere else to go,
To get a ladder, with which your love
Will climb up to see you at night:
I do all this hard work for your happiness,
But you shall do the hard work at night.
Go; I'll go to dinner; get to the Friar's.

JULIET	JULIET
Hie to high fortune! Honest nurse, farewell.	Wish me luck! Thank you nurse.
Exeunt	*Exit*

ORIGINAL TEXT	MODERN TRANSLATION
Friar Laurence's cell.	Friar Laurence's.
Enter FRIAR LAURENCE and ROMEO	*Enter FRIAR LAURENCE and ROMEO*
FRIAR LAURENCE So smile the heavens upon this holy act, That after hours with sorrow chide us not!	**FRIAR LAURENCE** I hope the heavens are happy with this marriage, So that bad things do not come of it!
ROMEO Amen, amen! but come what sorrow can, t cannot countervail the exchange of joy That one short minute gives me in her sight: Do thou but close our hands with holy words, Then love-devouring death do what he dare; It is enough I may but call her mine.	**ROMEO** I agree, I agree! But whatever bad thing comes, It can't outdo the happiness That I feel after seeing Juliet for one minute: Join us together in marriage, And death can do what it likes; As long as she is mine I am happy.
FRIAR LAURENCE These violent delights have violent ends And in their triumph die, like fire and powder, Which as they kiss consume: the sweetest honey Is loathsome in his own deliciousness And in the taste confounds the appetite: Therefore love moderately; long love doth so; Too swift arrives as tardy as too slow.	**FRIAR LAURENCE** Sudden happiness has a sudden ending And dies away like gunpowder and flame, Which meet like a kiss and explode: the sweetest honey Is horrible if you eat too much And will make you sick Therefore love in moderation, long lasting love does this; Love that is too quick is just as bad as love that is too slow.
Enter JULIET	*Enter JULIET*
Here comes the lady: O, so light a foot Will ne'er wear out the everlasting flint: A lover may bestride the gossamer That idles in the wanton summer air, And yet not fall; so light is vanity.	Here comes the lady: Oh she walks so lightly She'll never survive the difficult road of life: Those in love can walk on spider-web That floats in the summer air, And not fall; that's how surreal love is.
JULIET Good even to my ghostly confessor.	**JULIET** Good evening, my confessor.
FRIAR LAURENCE Romeo shall thank thee, daughter, for us both.	**FRIAR LAURENCE** Romeo shall be grateful enough for both of us.

JULIET As much to him, else is his thanks too much.	**JULIET** I shall be grateful too, so he doesn't thank too much.
ROMEO Ah, Juliet, if the measure of thy joy Be heap'd like mine and that thy skill be more To blazon it, then sweeten with thy breath This neighbour air, and let rich music's tongue Unfold the imagined happiness that both Receive in either by this dear encounter.	**ROMEO** Ah, Juliet, if the amount of joy you have is as big as mine, and you are better with words, then tell me Speak out How happy we will be in marriage.
JULIET Conceit, more rich in matter than in words, Brags of his substance, not of ornament: They are but beggars that can count their worth; But my true love is grown to such excess I cannot sum up sum of half my wealth.	**JULIET** My imagination is bigger than my words, But the love within me is so huge I cannot express even half of it.
FRIAR LAURENCE Come, come with me, and we will make short work; For, by your leaves, you shall not stay alone Till holy church incorporate two in one.	**FRIAR LAURENCE** Come, come with me, and we will do this quickly, I will not leave you alone until you are married.
Exeunt	*Exit*

Act 3 Scene 1

ORIGINAL TEXT	MODERN TRANSLATION
A public place.	A public place.
Enter MERCUTIO, BENVOLIO, Page, and Servants	*Enter MERCUTIO, BENVOLIO, Page, and Servants*
BENVOLIO I pray thee, good Mercutio, let's retire: The day is hot, the Capulets abroad, And, if we meet, we shall not scape a brawl; For now, these hot days, is the mad blood stirring.	**BENVOLIO** I beg you, Mercutio, let's leave: It's a hot day, the Capulets are around, And, if we meet them, we won't escape a fight; For in this hot weather, people become hot-headed.
MERCUTIO Thou art like one of those fellows that when he enters the confines of a tavern claps me his sword upon the table and says 'God send me no need of thee!' and by the operation of the second cup draws it on the drawer, when indeed there is no need.	**MERCUTIO** You are like one of those people that, when he walks into a pub, slaps his sword onto the table and says 'don't let me need to use you!' But by the second pint, pulls his sword out on the barman when there really is no need to.
BENVOLIO Am I like such a fellow?	**BENVOLIO** Am I like that?
MERCUTIO Come, come, thou art as hot a Jack in thy mood as any in Italy, and as soon moved to be moody, and as soon moody to be moved.	**MERCUTIO** Come one, you are as hot-headed as anyone in this country, and so easily wound up, that when you want to be angry you find something to get angry about.
BENVOLIO And what to?	**BENVOLIO** So what?
MERCUTIO Nay, an there were two such, we should have none shortly, for one would kill the other. Thou! why, thou wilt quarrel with a man that hath a hair more, or a hair less, in his beard, than thou hast: thou wilt quarrel with a man for cracking nuts, having no other reason but because thou hast hazel eyes: what	**MERCUTIO** If there were two men like you there would soon be none because you'd kill each other. You! You'd argue with a man over having one more or one less hair in his beard, than you have You would argue with a man for cracking nuts, Just because your eyes were the same colour as those nuts

eye but such an eye would spy out such a quarrel?	That's the kind of trouble seeking person you are.
Thy head is as fun of quarrels as an egg is full of meat, and yet thy head hath been beaten as addle as an egg for quarrelling: thou hast quarrelled with a man for coughing in the street, because he hath	Your head is full of anger like an egg is full of yolk, and yet your head has been beaten just like a scrambled egg. You have fought with a man for coughing in the street, because he
wakened thy dog that hath lain asleep in the sun:	woke up a dog which was sleeping in the sun:
didst thou not fall out with a tailor for wearing his new doublet before Easter? with another, for	Didn't you fall out with a tailor for wearing his clothes outside of the fashionable time? With someone else
tying his new shoes with old riband? and yet thou wilt tutor me from quarrelling!	for tying his new shoes up with old laces? And yet you try to teach me not to fight!

BENVOLIO

An I were so apt to quarrel as thou art, any man should buy the fee-simple of my life for an hour and a quarter.	If I were so keen on fighting as you are, My life insurance rates would be very high.

MERCUTIO

The fee-simple! O simple!	That's silly!

BENVOLIO

By my head, here come the Capulets.	Oh no, here come the Capulets.

MERCUTIO

By my heel, I care not.	I don't care.

Enter TYBALT and others

TYBALT

Follow me close, for I will speak to them. Gentlemen, good den: a word with one of you.	Back me up, I am going to speak to them. Men. Good afternoon: I want a word with one of you.

MERCUTIO

And but one word with one of us? couple it with something; make it a word and a blow.	Just one word? Put it together with something; say a word and blow.

TYBALT

You shall find me apt enough to that, sir, an you will give me occasion.	I am up for doing that, Just give me a reason.

MERCUTIO

Could you not take some occasion without giving?	Can't you find a reason without me giving it?

TYBALT

Mercutio, thou consort'st with Romeo,--	Mercutio, you hang around with Romeo..

MERCUTIO Consort! what, dost thou make us minstrels? an thou make minstrels of us, look to hear nothing but discords: here's my fiddlestick; here's that shall make you dance. 'Zounds, consort!	**MERCUTIO** 'Hang around'? Are you calling us musicians? You make musicians of us and you'll hear noise. Here's my instrument (touches his sword), it will make you dance! 'Hang out'!
BENVOLIO We talk here in the public haunt of men: Either withdraw unto some private place, And reason coldly of your grievances, Or else depart; here all eyes gaze on us.	**BENVOLIO** We are talking here in public, Either come somewhere quiet, And we will talk about this, Or leave; everyone is looking at us.
MERCUTIO Men's eyes were made to look, and let them gaze; I will not budge for no man's pleasure, I.	**MERCUTIO** That's what eyes are for, let them look; I'm not going anywhere.
Enter ROMEO	*Enter ROMEO*
TYBALT Well, peace be with you, sir: here comes my man.	**TYBALT** Calm down, sir: here comes the person I am looking for.
MERCUTIO But I'll be hanged, sir, if he wear your livery: Marry, go before to field, he'll be your follower; Your worship in that sense may call him 'man.'	**MERCUTIO** I'll be dead, if he's <u>your</u> man, If you run away, he will follow you. In that way you could call him your man.
TYBALT Romeo, the hate I bear thee can afford No better term than this,--thou art a villain.	**TYBALT** Romeo, the hate I have for you can express itself no better than this: you are a villain.
ROMEO Tybalt, the reason that I have to love thee Doth much excuse the appertaining rage To such a greeting: villain am I none; Therefore farewell; I see thou know'st me not.	**ROMEO** Tybalt, the reason I have to love you Excuses the anger I feel at your greeting; I am not a villain; So goodbye; it's clear you don't know me.
TYBALT Boy, this shall not excuse the injuries That thou hast done me; therefore turn and draw.	**TYBALT** Boy, this does not make up for the insults you have inflicted on me; turn around and pull out your sword.
ROMEO I do protest, I never injured thee, But love thee better than thou canst devise, Till thou shalt know the reason of my love: And so, good Capulet,--which name I tender	**ROMEO** I tell you, I never wronged you, But actually love you more than you can know, Until you know why I love you: So, good Capulet - a name I love

As dearly as my own,--be satisfied.

MERCUTIO
O calm, dishonourable, vile submission!
Alla stoccata carries it away.

Draws

Tybalt, you rat-catcher, will you walk?

TYBALT
What wouldst thou have with me?

MERCUTIO
Good king of cats, nothing but one of your nine
lives; that I mean to make bold withal, and as you
shall use me hereafter, drybeat the rest of the

eight. Will you pluck your sword out of his pitcher
by the ears? make haste, lest mine be about your
ears ere it be out.

TYBALT
I am for you.

Drawing

ROMEO
Gentle Mercutio, put thy rapier up.

MERCUTIO
Come, sir, your passado.

They fight

ROMEO
Draw, Benvolio; beat down their weapons.

Gentlemen, for shame, forbear this outrage!
Tybalt, Mercutio, the prince expressly hath
Forbidden bandying in Verona streets:
Hold, Tybalt! good Mercutio!

*TYBALT under ROMEO's arm stabs MERCUTIO, and
flies with his followers*

MERCUTIO
I am hurt.
A plague o' both your houses! I am sped.
Is he gone, and hath nothing?

As much as my own name..be satisfied.

MERCUTIO
Giving in like this is pathetic!
A swipe of my sword will stop it.

Pulls out sword

Tybalt, you scumbag, will you fight me?

TYBALT
What do you want with me?

MERCUTIO
King of cats, I want one of your nine
lives, I am planning on taking it, and
how you treat me after, shall decide what
happens to the other
eight. Will you pull out you sword?
Do it quick, else mine will be at your head
before you get yours out.

TYBALT
I will fight you.

Pulling out his sword

ROMEO
Mercutio, put your sword away.

MERCUTIO
Come on, show me forward stab.

They fight

ROMEO
Pull out your sword, Benvolio; hit their
weapons down.
Men, stop this!
Tybalt, Mercutio, the prince has
outlawed fighting in the streets of this city:
Stop, Tybalt! Mercutio!

*TYBALT stabs MERCUTIO whilst ROMEO is
holding him back. TYBALT and his men run
off.*

MERCUTIO
I am hurt.
Both of your families be cursed. I'm done.
Did he get away unhurt?

BENVOLIO
What, art thou hurt?

MERCUTIO
Ay, ay, a scratch, a scratch; marry, 'tis enough.
Where is my page? Go, villain, fetch a surgeon.

Exit Page

ROMEO
Courage, man; the hurt cannot be much.

MERCUTIO
No, 'tis not so deep as a well, nor so wide as a

church-door; but 'tis enough,'twill serve: ask for

me to-morrow, and you shall find me a grave man. I
am peppered, I warrant, for this world. A plague o'
both your houses! 'Zounds, a dog, a rat, a mouse, a
cat, to scratch a man to death! a braggart, a
rogue, a villain, that fights by the book of

arithmetic! Why the devil came you between us? I
was hurt under your arm.

ROMEO
I thought all for the best.

MERCUTIO
Help me into some house, Benvolio,
Or I shall faint. A plague o' both your houses!

They have made worms' meat of me: I have it,
And soundly too: your houses!

Exeunt MERCUTIO and BENVOLIO

ROMEO
This gentleman, the prince's near ally,

My very friend, hath got his mortal hurt

In my behalf; my reputation stain'd
With Tybalt's slander,--Tybalt, that an hour

Hath been my kinsman! O sweet Juliet,
Thy beauty hath made me effeminate

BENVOLIO
Are you hurt?

MERCUTIO
Just a scratch, but it's enough.
Where is my servant? Go, get a doctor.

Exit Page.

ROMEO
Be brave, it can't be too bad.

MERCUTIO
No, it's not as deep as a well or wide as
a

church-door, but it's enough. It will do;
ask for
me tomorrow and you will find I am dead.
I am done for this world. Both of your
families be cursed!
That pathetic animal, scratched me to
death! He learnt how to fight through
reading about it in a book!
Why did you get in-between us?
He stabbed me when you held me back.

ROMEO
I thought it was the right thing to do - to
try and stop the fight.

MERCUTIO
Help me into some house, Benvolio,
Or I shall faint. Cursed be both of your
families!
They have turned me into worm food: I am
done for. A curse on both Capulets and
Montagues.

Exit MERCUTIO and BENVOLIO

ROMEO
This man Mercutio, a close friend of the
Prince and
My good friend, has taken a wound which
will kill him
All for me; to protect my reputation
Which Tybalt was ruining - Tybalt, that
only for an hour
Has been my relative! Oh sweet Juliet,
Your beauty has made me weak

And in my temper soften'd valour's steel!

Re-enter BENVOLIO

BENVOLIO
O Romeo, Romeo, brave Mercutio's dead!
That gallant spirit hath aspired the clouds,
Which too untimely here did scorn the earth.

ROMEO
This day's black fate on more days doth depend;

This but begins the woe, others must end.

BENVOLIO
Here comes the furious Tybalt back again.

ROMEO
Alive, in triumph! and Mercutio slain!

Away to heaven, respective lenity,
And fire-eyed fury be my conduct now!

Re-enter TYBALT

Now, Tybalt, take the villain back again,
That late thou gavest me; for Mercutio's soul
Is but a little way above our heads,
Staying for thine to keep him company:
Either thou, or I, or both, must go with him.

TYBALT
Thou, wretched boy, that didst consort him here,

Shalt with him hence.

ROMEO
This shall determine that.

They fight; TYBALT falls

BENVOLIO
Romeo, away, be gone!
The citizens are up, and Tybalt slain.
Stand not amazed: the prince will doom thee death,

If thou art taken: hence, be gone, away!

ROMEO
O, I am fortune's fool!

And made my bravery go soft.

Re-enter BENVOLIO

BENVOLIO
Oh Romeo, Romeo, Mercutio is dead!
That brave man has gone to heaven,
He was too young to die.

ROMEO
The horrible events of today will affect the future;
The trouble that starts today will end in the future.

BENVOLIO
Here comes Tybalt back again.

ROMEO
Alive and celebrating! With Mercutio dead!
Goodbye mercy,
Anger take over me now!

Re-enter TYBALT

Now, Tybalt, call me villain again,
Like earlier; Mercutio's spirit
Has only just begun its journey to heaven,
Waiting for yours to join it:
Either you, or I, or both of us, must die.

TYBALT
You idiot boy, you hung around with him here,
And shall join him soon.

ROMEO
This fight will decide that.

They fight, ROMEO kills TYBALT

BENVOLIO
Romeo, get away, leave!
The public are up, and Tybalt is dead.
Don't stand there, the prince will have you killed,
If he catches you: so, go away!

ROMEO
My luck is so bad!

94

BENVOLIO
Why dost thou stay?

Exit ROMEO

Enter Citizens

First Citizen
Which way ran he that kill'd Mercutio?

Tybalt, that murderer, which way ran he?

BENVOLIO
There lies that Tybalt.

First Citizen
Up, sir, go with me;
I charge thee in the princes name, obey.

Enter Prince, attended; MONTAGUE, CAPULET, their Wives, and others

PRINCE
Where are the vile beginners of this fray?

BENVOLIO
O noble prince, I can discover all
The unlucky manage of this fatal brawl:
There lies the man, slain by young Romeo,
That slew thy kinsman, brave Mercutio.

LADY CAPULET
Tybalt, my cousin! O my brother's child!
O prince! O cousin! husband! O, the blood is spilt
O my dear kinsman! Prince, as thou art true,

For blood of ours, shed blood of Montague.
O cousin, cousin!

PRINCE
Benvolio, who began this bloody fray?

BENVOLIO
Tybalt, here slain, whom Romeo's hand did slay;

Romeo that spoke him fair, bade him bethink

How nice the quarrel was, and urged withal

Your high displeasure: all this uttered

BENVOLIO
Why are you staying here?

Exit ROMEO

Enter Citizens

First Citizen
Which way did he run who killed Mercutio?
Which way did Tybalt, the murderer, run?

BENVOLIO
There is Tybalt.

First Citizen
Get up man;
In the prince's name, do as I say.

Enter Prince, MONTAGUE, CAPULET, their Wives and others

PRINCE
Where are those who started this fight?

BENVOLIO
Prince, I can tell you all
About how this deadly fight took place:
There is the body of one killed by Romeo,
Who killed my friend, brave Mercutio.

LADY CAPULET
Tybalt, my cousin! Oh, my brother's child!
Oh prince! Oh cousin! Husband! Oh, the blood is spilt of my nephew! Prince, you are honest,
For this murder, kill a Montague.
Cousin, cousin!

PRINCE
Benvolio, who started this fight?

BENVOLIO
Tybalt, who lies here dead, who was then killed by Romeo;
Romeo; who spoke nicely to him, made him think
How silly the fight was, and begged him to avoid
your disapproval. He said all this

With gentle breath, calm look, knees humbly bow'd,
Could not take truce with the unruly spleen
Of Tybalt deaf to peace, but that he tilts
With piercing steel at bold Mercutio's breast,
Who all as hot, turns deadly point to point,
And, with a martial scorn, with one hand beats
Cold death aside, and with the other sends
It back to Tybalt, whose dexterity,
Retorts it: Romeo he cries aloud,
'Hold, friends! friends, part!' and, swifter than his tongue,
His agile arm beats down their fatal points,
And 'twixt them rushes; underneath whose arm
An envious thrust from Tybalt hit the life
Of stout Mercutio, and then Tybalt fled;
But by and by comes back to Romeo,
Who had but newly entertain'd revenge,
And to 't they go like lightning, for, ere I
Could draw to part them, was stout Tybalt slain.

And, as he fell, did Romeo turn and fly.
This is the truth, or let Benvolio die.

LADY CAPULET
He is a kinsman to the Montague;
Affection makes him false; he speaks not true:

Some twenty of them fought in this black strife,
And all those twenty could but kill one life.
I beg for justice, which thou, prince, must give;

Romeo slew Tybalt, Romeo must not live.

PRINCE
Romeo slew him, he slew Mercutio;

Who now the price of his dear blood doth owe?

MONTAGUE
Not Romeo, prince, he was Mercutio's friend;

His fault concludes but what the law should end,
The life of Tybalt.

PRINCE
And for that offence
Immediately we do exile him hence:
I have an interest in your hate's proceeding,
My blood for your rude brawls doth lie a-bleeding;
But I'll amerce you with so strong a fine
That you shall all repent the loss of mine:

calmly and gently, humbly
But could not calm down
Tybalt who was wild, and stabbed
his sword at brave Mercutio's chest,
Mercutio, angered, fought back,
And tried to
kill Tybalt.
Tybalt fought back.
Romeo shouted out
Stop friends, split it up! and, quicker than his tongue,
His arm beat down their swords,
He got between them: under his arm
Tybalt stabbed to death
Mercutio, and then Tybalt ran away;
But after a while came back to Romeo,
Who was now looking for revenge.
And they fought, before I
Could get between them, strong Tybalt was killed.
And, as he died, Romeo ran away.
This is the truth, I swear my life on it.

LADY CAPULET
He is a relative of Montague;
His love for Montagues will make him tell lies;
Around twenty men fought in this battle,
And it took all twenty to kill Tybalt.
I ask for justice, prince, and you must give it;
Romeo killed Tybalt, so Romeo must die.

PRINCE
Romeo killed Tybalt, Tybalt killed Mercutio;
Who is now to blame?

MONTAGUE
Not Romeo, prince, he was Mercutio's friend;
He did what the law would have done by killing Tybalt.

PRINCE
For that crime
He is exiled from this moment:
I am involved in this battle,
Mercutio was my relative,
I will punish you so severely
You shall be sorry for my loss:

I will be deaf to pleading and excuses; Nor tears nor prayers shall purchase out abuses: Therefore use none: let Romeo hence in haste, Else, when he's found, that hour is his last. Bear hence this body and attend our will: Mercy but murders, pardoning those that kill. *Exeunt*	I will not listen to begging or excuses; Not tears or prayers shall get you out of this: So use none: let Romeo get away quick, Else, when he's found, he shall die. Take this body away: Showing mercy to killers, only ends up with more murder. *Exit*

Act 3 Scene 2

ORIGINAL TEXT	MODERN ORIGINAL
Capulet's orchard.	Capulet's orchard.
Enter JULIET	*Enter JULIET*
JULIET	**JULIET**
Gallop apace, you fiery-footed steeds,	Hurry away, sun,
Towards Phoebus' lodging: such a wagoner	Towards your home for the night: the mythological
	Phaethon would drive you fast,
As Phaethon would whip you to the west,	And bring the night in right away.
And bring in cloudy night immediately.	Come and cover the sky, night,
Spread thy close curtain, love-performing night,	So that Romeo
That runaway's eyes may wink and Romeo	Can jump into my arms, hidden from everyone.
Leap to these arms, untalk'd of and unseen.	Lovers can make love
	in the dark; or if love is blind,
Lovers can see to do their amorous rites	It's best to do it at night. Come, night,
By their own beauties; or, if love be blind,	widow dressed in black,
It best agrees with night. Come, civil night,	And I will submit to Romeo,
Thou sober-suited matron, all in black,	And lose my virginity,
And learn me how to lose a winning match,	Let the shyness which makes me blush be
Play'd for a pair of stainless maidenhoods:	covered with you darkness, until sex
Hood my unmann'd blood, bating in my cheeks,	becomes natural,
With thy black mantle; till strange love, grown bold,	So I can do it honestly.
	Come night, come Romeo, my daytime in the night;
Think true love acted simple modesty.	
Come, night; come, Romeo; come, thou day in night;	You will lie upon the night
	Like snow on a raven's back.
For thou wilt lie upon the wings of night	Come, night, come, loving,
Whiter than new snow on a raven's back.	dark and black night,
Come, gentle night, come, loving, black-brow'd night,	Give me Romeo, and when he dies,
Give me my Romeo; and, when he shall die,	Make him into little stars
Take him and cut him out in little stars,	And he will make the night sky look beautiful
And he will make the face of heaven so fine	So all the world will be in love with the night
That all the world will be in love with night	And hate the sun.
	Oh, I have bought a whole house of love,
And pay no worship to the garish sun.	But not yet stepped foot in it; I am sold,
O, I have bought the mansion of a love,	But not yet enjoyed; so boring is today
But not possess'd it, and, though I am sold,	Just like the night before Christmas
Not yet enjoy'd: so tedious is this day	For an impatient child that has new clothes
As is the night before some festival	
To an impatient child that hath new robes	and isn't allowed to wear them. Oh, here comes the nurse,
And may not wear them. O, here comes my nurse,	And she brings news, and everyone who speaks
And she brings news; and every tongue that speaks	

But Romeo's name speaks heavenly eloquence.	Romeo's name is heavenly.
Enter Nurse, with cords	*Enter Nurse, with the rope ladder*
Now, nurse, what news? What hast thou there? the cords That Romeo bid thee fetch?	Now, nurse, what news? What have you there? The rope ladder that Romeo wanted you to get?
Nurse Ay, ay, the cords.	**Nurse** Yes, the rope ladder.
Throws them down	*Throws it down*
JULIET Ay me! what news? why dost thou wring thy hands?	**JULIET** What news? Why are you looking tense?
Nurse Ah, well-a-day! he's dead, he's dead, he's dead! We are undone, lady, we are undone! Alack the day! he's gone, he's kill'd, he's dead!	**Nurse** He's dead, he's dead, he's dead! It has ruined us, ruined us! What a terrible day! He has gone, he's killed, he's dead!
JULIET Can heaven be so envious?	**JULIET** Can heaven be so jealous?
Nurse Romeo can, Though heaven cannot: O Romeo, Romeo! Who ever would have thought it? Romeo!	**Nurse** Romeo can be hateful, But heaven can't. Oh Romeo, Romeo! Who would have thought it would be Romeo!
JULIET What devil art thou, that dost torment me thus? This torture should be roar'd in dismal hell. Hath Romeo slain himself? say thou but 'I,' And that bare vowel 'I' shall poison more Than the death-darting eye of cockatrice: I am not I, if there be such an I; Or those eyes shut, that make thee answer 'I.' If he be slain, say 'I'; or if not, no: Brief sounds determine of my weal or woe.	**JULIET** How evil are you, that you torture me like this? This is the torture of hell. Has Romeo killed himself? Say 'yes', And I will turn more poisonous that the deadly snake: I will not exist if Romeo has killed himself. Just tell me yes or no. Say it briefly so I will know if I am happy or sad.
Nurse I saw the wound, I saw it with mine eyes,-- God save the mark!--here on his manly breast: A piteous corse, a bloody piteous corse; Pale, pale as ashes, all bedaub'd in blood, All in gore-blood; I swounded at the sight.	**Nurse** I saw the wound, I saw it myself.. God bless that wound! Here on his Chest: A horrible wound, a bloody wound; Pale he was, covered in blood, All in blood, I fainted at the sight.

JULIET

O, break, my heart! poor bankrupt, break at once!

To prison, eyes, ne'er look on liberty!

Vile earth, to earth resign; end motion here;

And thou and Romeo press one heavy bier!

Nurse

O Tybalt, Tybalt, the best friend I had!
O courteous Tybalt! honest gentleman!
That ever I should live to see thee dead!

JULIET

What storm is this that blows so contrary?
Is Romeo slaughter'd, and is Tybalt dead?
My dear-loved cousin, and my dearer lord?
Then, dreadful trumpet, sound the general doom!
For who is living, if those two are gone?

Nurse

Tybalt is gone, and Romeo banished;
Romeo that kill'd him, he is banished.

JULIET

O God! did Romeo's hand shed Tybalt's blood?

Nurse

It did, it did; alas the day, it did!

JULIET

O serpent heart, hid with a flowering face!
Did ever dragon keep so fair a cave?
Beautiful tyrant! fiend angelical!
Dove-feather'd raven! wolvish-ravening lamb!

Despised substance of divinest show!
Just opposite to what thou justly seem'st,

A damned saint, an honourable villain!
O nature, what hadst thou to do in hell,
When thou didst bower the spirit of a fiend
In moral paradise of such sweet flesh?
Was ever book containing such vile matter

So fairly bound? O that deceit should dwell
In such a gorgeous palace!

JULIET

Oh, break, my heart! You've lost everything, so break!
My eyes go to prison, never to look again freely at anything!
Vile earth, I give my body to you; I will not move;
and me and Romeo can lie together in a coffin!

Nurse

Oh Tybalt, Tybalt, the best friend I had! Oh polite Tybalt! Honest man!
I cannot believe I am alive and you are dead!

JULIET

What is this message which is so different?
Is Romeo dead? and is Tybalt dead?
My cousin Tybalt and my master Romeo?
Then let the end of the world come!
For life is over if these two are dead.

Nurse

Tybalt is dead, Romeo banished;
Romeo killed him, so is banished.

JULIET

Oh God! Did Romeo kill Tybalt?

Nurse

Yes!

JULIET

Oh evil man disguised as beauty!
Did ever a monster seem so nice?
Beautiful tyrant! Evil angel!
Raven with feathers of a dove! Lamb that hunts like a wolf!
I hate him, but he seemed so amazing!
He is the opposite of what he seemed to be,
A cursed saint, an honest criminal!
Oh nature, what were you doing in hell.
When you did make this evil man
In such a perfect body?
Was there ever a book containing so much evil
Yet with a perfect cover? Oh that lies should live in such a stunning palace!

Nurse	**Nurse**
There's no trust,	There is nothing to trust,
No faith, no honesty in men; all perjured,	No honesty in men; all are liars,
All forsworn, all naught, all dissemblers.	All cheat and are wicked.
Ah, where's my man? give me some aqua vitae:	Where's Peter? Give me some alcohol:
These griefs, these woes, these sorrows make me old.	These sadness's make me feel old.
Shame come to Romeo!	Shame on Romeo!
JULIET	**JULIET**
Blister'd be thy tongue	May blisters grow on your tongue
For such a wish! he was not born to shame:	For wanting such a thing! He was not born to be shameful:
Upon his brow shame is ashamed to sit;	Shame is ashamed to rest on him;
For 'tis a throne where honour may be crown'd	For his head is a throne where honour can sit
Sole monarch of the universal earth.	
O, what a beast was I to chide at him!	Oh, how awful of me to be mad at him!
Nurse	**Nurse**
Will you speak well of him that kill'd your cousin?	Will you say nice things about the man who killed your cousin?
JULIET	**JULIET**
Shall I speak ill of him that is my husband?	Shall I speak badly of the man who is my husband?
Ah, poor my lord, what tongue shall smooth thy name,	Poor man, who shall speak well of you,
When I, thy three-hours wife, have mangled it?	When I, who have only been your wife a few hours, have criticised you?
But, wherefore, villain, didst thou kill my cousin?	But why, criminal, did you kill my cousin?
That villain cousin would have kill'd my husband:	Because my villain cousin would have killed you:
Back, foolish tears, back to your native spring;	Stop, tears, go back into my eyes;
Your tributary drops belong to woe,	I should cry with sadness,
Which you, mistaking, offer up to joy.	But I am crying with joy
My husband lives, that Tybalt would have slain;	Because Romeo is alive, who Tybalt would have killed;
And Tybalt's dead, that would have slain my husband:	And Tybalt's dead, who would have killed my husband:
All this is comfort; wherefore weep I then?	All this is good news, so why am I crying?
Some word there was, worser than Tybalt's death,	There was a word, worse than Tybalt's death.
That murder'd me: I would forget it fain;	That killed me: I wish I could forget it;
But, O, it presses to my memory,	But it sticks in my head,
Like damned guilty deeds to sinners' minds:	Like guilty actions do in sinners' minds:
'Tybalt is dead, and Romeo--banished;'	'Tybalt is dead, and Romeo...banished.'
That 'banished,' that one word 'banished,'	That one word 'banished'.
Hath slain ten thousand Tybalts. Tybalt's death	Is the same as killing ten thousand Tybalts. Tybalt's death
Was woe enough, if it had ended there:	was bad enough if it ended there:
Or, if sour woe delights in fellowship	But unhappiness loves company

And needly will be rank'd with other griefs,	And is joined by more unhappiness,
Why follow'd not, when she said 'Tybalt's dead,'	It would have been better after saying 'Tybalt's dead,'
Thy father, or thy mother, nay, or both,	That my dad or mum, or even both were dead too,
Which modern lamentations might have moved?	That would have made me sad.
But with a rear-ward following Tybalt's death,	But by following the news of Tybalt's death,
'Romeo is banished,' to speak that word,	With Romeo's banishment, to say that word,
Is father, mother, Tybalt, Romeo, Juliet,	Is the same as losing dad, mum, Tybalt, Romeo and myself all together, all dead.
All slain, all dead. 'Romeo is banished!'	'Romeo is banished!'
There is no end, no limit, measure, bound,	There is no end or limit
In that word's death; no words can that woe sound.	In the unhappiness caused by that word; no words can be as bad.
Where is my father, and my mother, nurse?	Where are my mum and dad, nurse?
Nurse	**Nurse**
Weeping and wailing over Tybalt's corse:	Crying and grieving over Tybalt's dead body:
Will you go to them? I will bring you thither.	Do you want to go to them? I will take you.
JULIET	**JULIET**
Wash they his wounds with tears: mine shall be spent,	His wounds will be washed with their tears: mine shall be used,
When theirs are dry, for Romeo's banishment.	When theirs are finished, for Romeo's banishment.
Take up those cords: poor ropes, you are beguiled,	Take this rope ladder, it is useless,
Both you and I; for Romeo is exiled:	just like I am; because Romeo is exiled:
He made you for a highway to my bed;	He made the ladder as a road to my bed
But I, a maid, die maiden-widowed.	But I, a virgin, will die a virgin.
Come, cords, come, nurse; I'll to my wedding-bed;	Come ropes, come, nurse; I will go to my wedding-bed;
And death, not Romeo, take my maidenhead!	And death, not Romeo, will take my virginity.
Nurse	**Nurse**
Hie to your chamber: I'll find Romeo	Go to your room: I'll find Romeo
To comfort you: I wot well where he is.	To comfort you: I know where he is.
Hark ye, your Romeo will be here at night:	Listen, Romeo will be here tonight:
I'll to him; he is hid at Laurence' cell.	I'll find him; he is hidden at Friar Laurence's.
JULIET	**JULIET**
O, find him! give this ring to my true knight,	Oh find him! Give him this ring.
And bid him come to take his last farewell.	And ask him to come and say his final goodbye.
Exeunt	*Exit*

ORIGINAL TEXT	MODERN TRANSLATION
Friar Laurence's cell.	Friar Laurence's cell.
Enter FRIAR LAURENCE	*Enter FRIAR LAURENCE*
FRIAR LAURENCE Romeo, come forth; come forth, thou fearful man: Affliction is enamour'd of thy parts, And thou art wedded to calamity.	**FRIAR LAURENCE** Romeo, come here; come here, you fearful man: Problems seem to like you, And you are married to trouble.
Enter ROMEO	*Enter ROMEO*
ROMEO Father, what news? what is the prince's doom? What sorrow craves acquaintance at my hand, That I yet know not?	**ROMEO** Father, what news? What has the prince decided? What sadness wants to join me, That I don't yet know about?
FRIAR LAURENCE Too familiar Is my dear son with such sour company: I bring thee tidings of the prince's doom.	**FRIAR LAURENCE** Too familiar are you with such sadness: I bring you news of the prince's decision.
ROMEO What less than dooms-day is the prince's doom?	**ROMEO** What less is the prince's decision than my own death?
FRIAR LAURENCE A gentler judgment vanish'd from his lips, Not body's death, but body's banishment.	**FRIAR LAURENCE** A less severe punishment has been announced, Not death, but banishment.
ROMEO Ha, banishment! be merciful, say 'death;' For exile hath more terror in his look, Much more than death: do not say 'banishment.'	**ROMEO** Ha, banishment! Be kind and say 'death;' Because being exiled is worse, Than death: do not say 'banishment.'
FRIAR LAURENCE Hence from Verona art thou banished: Be patient, for the world is broad and wide.	**FRIAR LAURENCE** From this city you are banished: Be patient, the world is a big place.
ROMEO There is no world without Verona walls, But purgatory, torture, hell itself. Hence-banished is banish'd from the world,	**ROMEO** There is no world outside this city, But torture and hell. So being banished from Verona is being banished from the world,

Original	Modern
And world's exile is death: then banished,	And being banished from the world is
Is death mis-term'd: calling death banishment,	death, So it's death by a different name,
Thou cutt'st my head off with a golden axe,	You cut off my head
And smilest upon the stroke that murders me.	And smile over the thing that kills me.
FRIAR LAURENCE	**FRIAR LAURENCE**
O deadly sin! O rude unthankfulness!	Oh rude and ungrateful man!
Thy fault our law calls death; but the kind prince,	What you did wrong, the law says you
	should die for, but the kind prince,
Taking thy part, hath rush'd aside the law,	Taking your side, has ignored the law,
And turn'd that black word death to banishment:	And changed death to banishment:
This is dear mercy, and thou seest it not.	This is merciful of him, but you don't see
	it.
ROMEO	**ROMEO**
'Tis torture, and not mercy: heaven is here,	It's torture, not mercy: heaven is here,
Where Juliet lives; and every cat and dog	Where Juliet lives; every cat and dog
And little mouse, every unworthy thing,	And house, every little thing,
Live here in heaven and may look on her;	Living here in heaven can look at her;
But Romeo may not: more validity,	But I may not: more authority,
More honourable state, more courtship lives	More honour, more applause goes to
In carrion-flies than Romeo: they my seize	flies than Romeo: they may grab
On the white wonder of dear Juliet's hand	Onto the hand of Juliet
And steal immortal blessing from her lips,	And steal blessing from her lips,
Who even in pure and vestal modesty,	Juliet is so pure and shy,
Still blush, as thinking their own kisses sin;	She blushed when we kiss, thinking it is
	wrong;
But Romeo may not; he is banished:	But Romeo may not, he is banished:
Flies may do this, but I from this must fly:	Flies can do it, but I must fly away:
They are free men, but I am banished.	They are free, but I am banished.
And say'st thou yet that exile is not death?	And you say exile is not death?
Hadst thou no poison mix'd, no sharp-ground knife,	If you had poison or a sharp knife,
No sudden mean of death, though ne'er so mean,	To kill me, you wouldn't be so mean,
But 'banished' to kill me?--'banished'?	But 'banished' to kill me? 'Banished'?
O friar, the damned use that word in hell;	Oh Friar, that word can go to hell;
Howlings attend it: how hast thou the heart,	It's evil: how can you,
Being a divine, a ghostly confessor,	Being a priest, a confessor,
A sin-absolver, and my friend profess'd,	A sin-forgiver and my friend,
To mangle me with that word 'banished'?	Ruin me with the word 'banished'?
FRIAR LAURENCE	**FRIAR LAURENCE**
Thou fond mad man, hear me but speak a word.	You mad man, let me say something.
ROMEO	**ROMEO**
O, thou wilt speak again of banishment.	Oh, you will speak again of banishment.
FRIAR LAURENCE	**FRIAR LAURENCE**
I'll give thee armour to keep off that word:	I'll give you protection from the word:
Adversity's sweet milk, philosophy,	The antidote to trouble: philosophy,
To comfort thee, though thou art banished.	To comfort you, even though you are
	banished.

ROMEO

Yet 'banished'? Hang up philosophy!

Unless philosophy can make a Juliet,
Displant a town, reverse a prince's doom,
It helps not, it prevails not: talk no more.

FRIAR LAURENCE

O, then I see that madmen have no ears.

ROMEO

How should they, when that wise men have no
eyes?

FRIAR LAURENCE

Let me dispute with thee of thy estate.

ROMEO

Thou canst not speak of that thou dost not feel:
Wert thou as young as I, Juliet thy love,

An hour but married, Tybalt murdered,
Doting like me and like me banished,
Then mightst thou speak, then mightst thou tear thy
hair,
And fall upon the ground, as I do now,
Taking the measure of an unmade grave.

Knocking within

FRIAR LAURENCE

Arise; one knocks; good Romeo, hide thyself.

ROMEO

Not I; unless the breath of heartsick groans,
Mist-like, infold me from the search of eyes.

Knocking

FRIAR LAURENCE

Hark, how they knock! Who's there? Romeo, arise;

Thou wilt be taken. Stay awhile! Stand up;

Knocking

ROMEO

You're still going on about 'banished'?
Forget philosophy!
Unless philosophy can make a Juliet,
pick up a town and drop it somewhere
else, or reverse a prince's decision,
It doesn't help. Say no more.

FRIAR LAURENCE

Oh, I see madmen cannot listen.

ROMEO

How should they, when wise men can't
see?

FRIAR LAURENCE

Let me talk with you about your situation.

ROMEO

You can't speak about what you don't feel:
If you were as young as I am, and Juliet
your love,
Only married an hour, Tybalt murdered,
In love like me yet banished,
Then you could speak, you might
tear your hair out,
Fall down on the ground, like I do now,
Measuring out the grave which hasn't yet
been dug.

There is a knock at the door

FRIAR LAURENCE

Get up, someone's knocking; Romeo, hide.

ROMEO

I won't hide, unless my unhappy groans,
Create a mist which covers me from
people's eyes.

More knocking

FRIAR LAURENCE

Listen, how they knock! Who's there?
Romeo, get up;
You will be taken. Stay here a bit, Stand
up;

More knocking

Run to my study. By and by! God's will,
What simpleness is this! I come, I come!

Knocking

Who knocks so hard? whence come you? what's
your will?

Nurse
[Within] Let me come in, and you shall know
my errand;
I come from Lady Juliet.

FRIAR LAURENCE
Welcome, then.

Enter Nurse

Nurse
O holy friar, O, tell me, holy friar,
Where is my lady's lord, where's Romeo?

FRIAR LAURENCE
There on the ground, with his own tears made
drunk.

Nurse
O, he is even in my mistress' case,
Just in her case! O woful sympathy!
Piteous predicament! Even so lies she,
Blubbering and weeping, weeping and blubbering.

Stand up, stand up; stand, and you be a man:
For Juliet's sake, for her sake, rise and stand;
Why should you fall into so deep an O?

ROMEO
Nurse!

Nurse
Ah sir! ah sir! Well, death's the end of all.

ROMEO
Spakest thou of Juliet? how is it with her?
Doth she not think me an old murderer,
Now I have stain'd the childhood of our joy

With blood removed but little from her own?

Where is she? and how doth she? and what says

Run to my office. Wait a minute! For God's
sake, you are being so stupid! I'm coming!

More knocking

Who is that knocking so hard? Where do
you come from and what do you want?

Nurse
Let me come in and I shall tell you why I
am here;
I've come from Juliet.

FRIAR LAURENCE
Then you are welcome.

Enter Nurse

Nurse
Oh holy priest, oh tell me,
Where is Romeo?

FRIAR LAURENCE
There on the ground, intoxicated by his
own tears.

Nurse
Oh, he is the same as Juliet,
Just like her! Oh how sad!
A terrible situation! She lies just like that,
Crying and blubbering, crying and
blubbering.
Stand up and be a man:
For Juliet's sake, stand up;
Why should you be so sad?

ROMEO
Nurse!

Nurse
Ah sir, well death ends it for us all.

ROMEO
Have you spoken about Juliet? How is she?
Does she think I am a murderer,
Now I have stained the start of our
happiness
With blood that is related closely to her
own?
Where is she, and how is she? What does
she say

My conceal'd lady to our cancell'd love?	My hidden wife, about our ruined love?
Nurse O, she says nothing, sir, but weeps and weeps; And now falls on her bed; and then starts up, And Tybalt calls; and then on Romeo cries, And then down falls again.	**Nurse** She says nothing, just cries and cries; And then falls on her bed; and then gets up, And shouts Tybalt's name, then your name, Then falls down again.
ROMEO As if that name, Shot from the deadly level of a gun, Did murder her; as that name's cursed hand Murder'd her kinsman. O, tell me, friar, tell me, In what vile part of this anatomy Doth my name lodge? tell me, that I may sack The hateful mansion.	**ROMEO** As if my name, Shot like a bullet from a gun, Did kill her; just like I did Kill her cousin. Oh tell me, Friar, tell me, In what part of my body is my name kept? Tell me, so I can cut it out.
Drawing his sword	*Pulling out his sword*
FRIAR LAURENCE Hold thy desperate hand: Art thou a man? thy form cries out thou art: Thy tears are womanish; thy wild acts denote The unreasonable fury of a beast: Unseemly woman in a seeming man! Or ill-beseeming beast in seeming both! Thou hast amazed me· by my holy order, I thought thy disposition better temper'd. Hast thou slain Tybalt? wilt thou slay thyself? nd stay thy lady too that lives in thee, By doing damned hate upon thyself? Why rail'st thou on thy birth, the heaven, and earth? Since birth, and heaven, and earth, all three do meet In thee at once; which thou at once wouldst lose. Fie, fie, thou shamest thy shape, thy love, thy wit; Which, like a usurer, abound'st in all, And usest none in that true use indeed Which should bedeck thy shape, thy love, thy wit: Thy noble shape is but a form of wax, Digressing from the valour of a man; Thy dear love sworn but hollow perjury,	**FRIAR LAURENCE** Stop your desperate actions: Are you a man? You look like one: But cry like a woman; your crazy actions show You are like a wild animal: You act like a woman inside a man's body! Or are a wild animal! You shock me I thought I knew your personality better. Have you killed Tybalt? Will you kill yourself? And would you kill Juliet who is joined to you, By killing yourself? Why moan about your birth, heaven and earth? Since birth, heaven and earth do all meet together in you at the same time, but you'd throw it all away. You bring shame to man, Juliet and your intelligence; You have so much intelligence, And use none of it here where it is needed Your body is like a wax statue, Without the honour a man should have; The love you swore on is shallow and untrue,

Killing that love which thou hast vow'd to cherish;	You are killing the love you promised to protect;
Thy wit, that ornament to shape and love,	Your intelligence, supposed to guide you in love,
Misshapen in the conduct of them both,	Is not working properly here,
Like powder in a skitless soldier's flask,	Like gunpowder belonging to a careless soldier,
Is set afire by thine own ignorance,	Explodes because of his own stupidity,
And thou dismember'd with thine own defence.	You break apart the thing which should save you.
What, rouse thee, man! thy Juliet is alive,	Snap out of it man! Juliet is alive,
For whose dear sake thou wast but lately dead;	For her you were nearly killed earlier today;
There art thou happy: Tybalt would kill thee,	Thus should make you happy: Tybalt wanted to kill you,
But thou slew'st Tybalt; there are thou happy too:	But you killed Tybalt; this should make you happy too:
The law that threaten'd death becomes thy friend	The law that looked like it would end your life has become your friend
And turns it to exile; there art thou happy:	And now you are only exiled; this should make you happy:
A pack of blessings lights up upon thy back;	Lots of good things have happened to you;
Happiness courts thee in her best array;	Happiness is all over you;
But, like a misbehaved and sullen wench,	But like a spoilt little girl,
Thou pout'st upon thy fortune and thy love:	You sulk about your bad luck and love:
Take heed, take heed, for such die miserable.	Listen, listen, those kind of people die miserable.
Go, get thee to thy love, as was decreed,	Go, get to Juliet, as was planned,
Ascend her chamber, hence and comfort her:	Climb into her bedroom and comfort her:
But look thou stay not till the watch be set,	But don't stay too late when the guards are out,
For then thou canst not pass to Mantua;	Else it will be too late to pass to the city of Mantua;
Where thou shalt live, till we can find a time	Where you shall live, until we can find a time
To blaze your marriage, reconcile your friends,	To make your marriage public, rejoin you with your friends,
Beg pardon of the prince, and call thee back	Ask the prince's forgiveness, and call you back
With twenty hundred thousand times more joy	With thousands of times more happiness
Than thou went'st forth in lamentation.	Than you went away with in sadness.
Go before, nurse: commend me to thy lady;	Go ahead, nurse: tell Juliet I said hi;
And bid her hasten all the house to bed,	And tell her to get everyone to bed,
Which heavy sorrow makes them apt unto:	Which sadness makes people want to do:
Romeo is coming.	Romeo is coming.
Nurse	**Nurse**
O Lord, I could have stay'd here all the night	Oh I could have stayed here all night
To hear good counsel: O, what learning is!	to hear good advice: education is so amazing!

My lord, I'll tell my lady you will come.	I will tell Juliet you are coming.
ROMEO Do so, and bid my sweet prepare to chide.	**ROMEO** Do that, and tell her to get ready to tell me off.
Nurse Here, sir, a ring she bid me give you, sir: Hie you, make haste, for it grows very late.	**Nurse** Here is a ring she wanted me to give to you: Hurry up, it's getting late.
Exit	*Exit*
ROMEO How well my comfort is revived by this!	**ROMEO** I feel so much better now!
FRIAR LAURENCE Go hence; good night; and here stands all your state: Either be gone before the watch be set, Or by the break of day disguised from hence: Sojourn in Mantua; I'll find out your man, And he shall signify from time to time Every good hap to you that chances here: Give me thy hand; 'tis late: farewell; good night.	**FRIAR LAURENCE** Go now, good night; here is the situation: Either be gone before the guards come out, Or in the morning leave in disguise; Rest in the city of Mantua; I'll find your friend, And he'll update you every now and then Every bit of news about your situation: Give me your hand, it's late - goodbye and goodnight.
ROMEO But that a joy past joy calls out on me, It were a grief, so brief to part with thee: Farewell.	**ROMEO** If it wasn't for the happiness I'm going to, I'd be sad to leave you. Goodbye.
Exeunt	*Exit*

ORIGINAL TEXT	MODERN TRANSLATION
A room in Capulet's house.	A room in Capulet's house.
Enter CAPULET, LADY CAPULET, and PARIS	*Enter CAPULET, LADY CAPULET, and PARIS*
CAPULET Things have fall'n out, sir, so unluckily, That we have had no time to move our daughter: Look you, she loved her kinsman Tybalt dearly, And so did I:--Well, we were born to die. 'Tis very late, she'll not come down to-night: I promise you, but for your company, I would have been a-bed an hour ago.	**CAPULET** Things have turned out, sir, so unluckily, That we have not had time to persuade our daughter to marry you; Look, she loved her cousin Tybalt very much, And so did I: We were all born to die though. It's very late, she will not be coming downstairs tonight: If it weren't for the fact that you are here, I would have gone to bed an hour ago myself.
PARIS These times of woe afford no time to woo. Madam, good night: commend me to your daughter.	**PARIS** This time of sadness allows no time for love. Lady, goodnight: say hello to your daughter from me.
LADY CAPULET I will, and know her mind early to-morrow; To-night she is mew'd up to her heaviness.	**LADY CAPULET** I will, and early tomorrow we will know her decision; Tonight she is alone with her sadness.
CAPULET Sir Paris, I will make a desperate tender Of my child's love: I think she will be ruled In all respects by me; nay, more, I doubt it not. Wife, go you to her ere you go to bed; Acquaint her here of my son Paris' love; And bid her, mark you me, on Wednesday next-- But, soft! what day is this?	**CAPULET** Paris, I will make a strong argument For my child's love; I think she will do what I tell her, in fact I do not doubt it. Wife, go and see her before going to bed; Tell her how much Paris loves her; And ask her to, next Wednesday... Hang on, what day is it today?
PARIS Monday, my lord,	**PARIS** Monday.
CAPULET Monday! ha, ha! Well, Wednesday is too soon, O' Thursday let it be: o' Thursday, tell her, She shall be married to this noble earl.	**CAPULET** Monday! ha, ha! Well Wednesday is too soon, On Thursday let it be, on Thursday, tell her, She shall marry Paris.

Original	Modern
Will you be ready? do you like this haste?	Will you be ready Paris? Do you like doing it this quick?
We'll keep no great ado,--a friend or two;	We'll not have a huge wedding - just a friend or two;
For, hark you, Tybalt being slain so late,	Because, listen, with Tybalt having been killed so recently,
It may be thought we held him carelessly,	It might be thought we didn't care about him,
Being our kinsman, if we revel much:	Being a relative, if we party too hard:
Therefore we'll have some half a dozen friends,	So we will have a half dozen friends,
And there an end. But what say you to Thursday?	And that's it. What do you say to Thursday?
PARIS	**PARIS**
My lord, I would that Thursday were to-morrow.	I wish it were Thursday tomorrow.
CAPULET	**CAPULET**
Well get you gone: o' Thursday be it, then.	Well you get going: On Thursday it will be, then.
Go you to Juliet ere you go to bed,	Wife, go to Juliet before you go to bed,
Prepare her, wife, against this wedding-day.	Prepare her for her wedding day.
Farewell, my lord. Light to my chamber, ho!	Goodbye, my lord. Send lights to my bedroom.
Afore me! it is so very very late,	Before me! It is so so late,
That we may call it early by and by.	We may as well call it early morning.
Good night.	Good night.
Exeunt	*Exit*

Act 3 Scene 5

ORIGINAL TEXT	MODERN TRANSLATION
Capulet's orchard.	Capulet's orchard.
Enter ROMEO and JULIET above, at the window	*Enter ROMEO and JULIET above, at the window*
JULIET Wilt thou be gone? it is not yet near day: It was the nightingale, and not the lark, That pierced the fearful hollow of thine ear; Nightly she sings on yon pomegranate-tree: Believe me, love, it was the nightingale.	**JULIET** Are you going? It's not near morning yet: That was the night bird singing, not the bird of morning, That you heard in your ear; She sings each night on that tree over there: Believe me, love, it was the nightingale.
ROMEO It was the lark, the herald of the morn, No nightingale: look, love, what envious streaks Do lace the severing clouds in yonder east: Night's candles are burnt out, and jocund day Stands tiptoe on the misty mountain tops. I must be gone and live, or stay and die.	**ROMEO** It was the lark, the signal of morning, No nightingale: look, love, what jealous streaks of light are coming through the clouds in the east: The night lights are gone, and day Is just about to come over the mountains. I must be gone to stay alive, or stay here and die.
JULIET Yon light is not day-light, I know it, I: It is some meteor that the sun exhales, To be to thee this night a torch-bearer, And light thee on thy way to Mantua: Therefore stay yet; thou need'st not to be gone.	**JULIET** That light is not daylight, I know it, It is a meteor coming out of the sun, Which is going to be a light to guide you, On your way to Mantua: So stay a bit: you don't need to be gone.
ROMEO Let me be ta'en, let me be put to death; I am content, so thou wilt have it so. I'll say yon grey is not the morning's eye, 'Tis but the pale reflex of Cynthia's brow; Nor that is not the lark, whose notes do beat The vaulty heaven so high above our heads: I have more care to stay than will to go: Come, death, and welcome! Juliet wills it so. How is't, my soul? let's talk; it is not day.	**ROMEO** Let me be captured and killed; I am happy, if that's what you want. I will say the light over there is not morning, It's the reflection of the moon; And that is not the lark, whose singing I hear Up in the sky: I want to stay more than I want to go: Come, death, you are welcome! Juliet wants it. How are you, my soul? Let's talk: it's not day.

JULIET
It is, it is: hie hence, be gone, away!
It is the lark that sings so out of tune,
Straining harsh discords and unpleasing sharps.
Some say the lark makes sweet division;

This doth not so, for she divideth us:
Some say the lark and loathed toad change eyes,

O, now I would they had changed voices too!
Since arm from arm that voice doth us affray,
Hunting thee hence with hunt's-up to the day,
O, now be gone; more light and light it grows.

ROMEO
More light and light; more dark and dark our woes!

Enter Nurse, to the chamber

Nurse
Madam!

JULIET
Nurse?

Nurse
Your lady mother is coming to your chamber:
The day is broke; be wary, look about.

Exit

JULIET
Then, window, let day in, and let life out.

ROMEO
Farewell, farewell! one kiss, and I'll descend.

He goeth down

JULIET
Art thou gone so? love, lord, ay, husband, friend!

I must hear from thee every day in the hour,
For in a minute there are many days:

O, by this count I shall be much in years
Ere I again behold my Romeo!

ROMEO
Farewell!

JULIET
It is, it is: be gone, go!
It is the morning bird that sings so badly,
Straining horrible notes.
Some say the lark makes a nice division
between day and night;
This is not true, because she splits us up:
Some say the lark and the today change
eyes (*this was an old folktale*),
Oh I wish they had changed voices too!
Since that voice does split us up,
The men will be hunting soon,
Oh be gone; it's getting lighter.

ROMEO
The lighter it gets, the darker our troubles!

Enter Nurse, to Juliet's bedroom.

Nurse
Madam!

JULIET
Nurse?

Nurse
Your mum is on her way to your bedroom:
It is morning, be careful, look about.

Exit

JULIET
Then, window, let day in and life out.

ROMEO
Goodbye, goodbye! One kiss and I will
climb down.

He climbs down

JULIET
Are you gone like that? Yes, husband,
friend!
I must hear from you every day,
Minutes will pass by so slowly without
you:
By this count I shall be very old
Before I see Romeo again.

ROMEO
Goodbye!

I will omit no opportunity
That may convey my greetings, love, to thee.

JULIET
O think'st thou we shall ever meet again?

ROMEO
I doubt it not; and all these woes shall serve
For sweet discourses in our time to come.

JULIET
O God, I have an ill-divining soul!
Methinks I see thee, now thou art below,
As one dead in the bottom of a tomb:
Either my eyesight fails, or thou look'st pale.

ROMEO
And trust me, love, in my eye so do you:
Dry sorrow drinks our blood. Adieu, adieu!

Exit

JULIET
O fortune, fortune! all men call thee fickle:

If thou art fickle, what dost thou with him.

That is renown'd for faith? Be fickle, fortune;
For then, I hope, thou wilt not keep him long,

But send him back.

LADY CAPULET
[Within] Ho, daughter! are you up?

JULIET
Who is't that calls? is it my lady mother?
Is she not down so late, or up so early?
What unaccustom'd cause procures her hither?

Enter LADY CAPULET

LADY CAPULET
Why, how now, Juliet!

JULIET
Madam, I am not well.

I will miss no opportunity
To send you a message of love.

JULIET
Do you think we will ever meet again?

ROMEO
I don't doubt it; and all this sadness
Will be stories to tell in our future lives.

JULIET
Oh God, I see into the future!
I see you, now you are below,
As one dead in a grave:
Either my eyes are playing up, or you look
pale.

ROMEO
And trust me, love, you love pale to me:
Sadness makes us unwell. Goodbye,
goodbye!

Exit

JULIET
Oh luck, luck! All men say you can't make
your mind up:
If that's true, what are you doing with
Romeo
Who is so faithful? Be fickle, luck;
Then, I hope, you will not keep Romeo
long,
But send him back to me.

LADY CAPULET
(outside the bedroom) Daughter! Are you
up?

JULIET
Who is that calling? Is it my mother?
Isn't it late to be up, or early to be up?
What odd reason make her come here?

Enter LADY CAPULET

LADY CAPULET
What's happening, Juliet!

JULIET
I am not well.

LADY CAPULET Evermore weeping for your cousin's death? What, wilt thou wash him from his grave with tears? An if thou couldst, thou couldst not make him live; Therefore, have done: some grief shows much of love; But much of grief shows still some want of wit.	**LADY CAPULET** Still crying about Tybalt's death? Will your tears make him come back to life? And if you could, you couldn't bring him back to life; So stop crying: your sadness shows how much you loved him; But too much sadness suggests you are a bit stupid.
JULIET Yet let me weep for such a feeling loss.	**JULIET** Let me cry over my loss.
LADY CAPULET So shall you feel the loss, but not the friend Which you weep for.	**LADY CAPULET** You will feel the sadness of the loss, but Tybalt will feel nothing.
JULIET Feeling so the loss, Cannot choose but ever weep the friend.	**JULIET** Feeling sad over losing him, I cannot help by cry.
LADY CAPULET Well, girl, thou weep'st not so much for his death, As that the villain lives which slaughter'd him.	**LADY CAPULET** Well girl, you cry not so much for his Tybalt's death, As for the one who killed him.
JULIET What villain madam?	**JULIET** Who do you mean?
LADY CAPULET That same villain, Romeo.	**LADY CAPULET** The villain, Romeo.
JULIET [Aside] Villain and he be many miles asunder.-- God Pardon him! I do, with all my heart; And yet no man like he doth grieve my heart.	**JULIET** (quietly) He is nothing like a villain... God forgive him! I do completely; And yet no-one makes me sad like him.
LADY CAPULET That is, because the traitor murderer lives.	**LADY CAPULET** I mean, you cry because the murderer is still alive.
JULIET Ay, madam, from the reach of these my hands: Would none but I might venge my cousin's death!	**JULIET** Yes, he is beyond my reach: I would love to gain revenge for Tybalt's death!
LADY CAPULET We will have vengeance for it, fear thou not: Then weep no more. I'll send to one in Mantua,	**LADY CAPULET** We will get revenge, don't you worry: Now stop crying. I will send someone to Mantua,

Where that same banish'd runagate doth live,
Shall give him such an unaccustom'd dram,
That he shall soon keep Tybalt company:
And then, I hope, thou wilt be satisfied.

JULIET
Indeed, I never shall be satisfied
With Romeo, till I behold him--dead--
Is my poor heart for a kinsman vex'd.
Madam, if you could find out but a man
To bear a poison, I would temper it;
That Romeo should, upon receipt thereof,
Soon sleep in quiet. O, how my heart abhors
To hear him named, and cannot come to him.
To wreak the love I bore my cousin
Upon his body that slaughter'd him!

LADY CAPULET
Find thou the means, and I'll find such a man.
But now I'll tell thee joyful tidings, girl.

JULIET
And joy comes well in such a needy time:
What are they, I beseech your ladyship?

LADY CAPULET
Well, well, thou hast a careful father, child;
One who, to put thee from thy heaviness,
Hath sorted out a sudden day of joy,
That thou expect'st not nor I look'd not for.

JULIET
Madam, in happy time, what day is that?

LADY CAPULET
Marry, my child, early next Thursday morn,

The gallant, young and noble gentleman,
The County Paris, at Saint Peter's Church,
Shall happily make thee there a joyful bride.

JULIET
Now, by Saint Peter's Church and Peter too,
He shall not make me there a joyful bride.
I wonder at this haste; that I must wed

Ere he, that should be husband, comes to woo.
I pray you, tell my lord and father, madam,
I will not marry yet; and, when I do, I swear,
It shall be Romeo, whom you know I hate,

Where Romeo lives,
To poison his drink,
So that he will be dead like Tybalt:
Then, I hope, you will be satisfied.

JULIET
I shall never be satisfied
With Romeo, until I see him...dead...
Dead is how my heart feels.
If you could find a man
To take a poison, I'd mix it myself;
So Romeo should, after drinking it,
Soon be dead. I hate
To hear his name, and I can't go to him.
To take the love I had for Tybalt
Out upon Romeo's body!

LADY CAPULET
You find the way and I will find the person.
But now I have good news, girl.

JULIET
I need some good news,
What is it?

LADY CAPULET
Well, your father, child;
To stop you being unhappy,
Have arranged a day of joy,
That you were not expecting or looking
for.

JULIET
What day is that?

LADY CAPULET
To be married, my child, next Thursday
morning,
To the young and wonderful man,
Paris, at Saint Peter's Church,
Where he shall make you a happy wife.

JULIET
I swear by Saint Peter and his Church,
He shall not make me a happy wife.
I am confused at this rushing; that I must
marry
Before Paris even comes to pursue me.
I beg you, tell my dad,
I will not marry yet; and, when I do, I
promise,

Rather than Paris. These are news indeed!

LADY CAPULET
Here comes your father; tell him so yourself,
And see how he will take it at your hands.

Enter CAPULET and Nurse

CAPULET
When the sun sets, the air doth drizzle dew;
But for the sunset of my brother's son
It rains downright.
How now! a conduit, girl? what, still in tears?
Evermore showering? In one little body
Thou counterfeit'st a bark, a sea, a wind;
For still thy eyes, which I may call the sea,
Do ebb and flow with tears; the bark thy body is,
Sailing in this salt flood; the winds, thy sighs;
Who, raging with thy tears, and they with them,

Without a sudden calm, will overset
Thy tempest-tossed body. How now, wife!

Have you deliver'd to her our decree?

LADY CAPULET
Ay, sir; but she will none, she gives you thanks.

I would the fool were married to her grave!

CAPULET
Soft! take me with you, take me with you, wife.
How! will she none? doth she not give us thanks?
Is she not proud? doth she not count her blest,

Unworthy as she is, that we have wrought
So worthy a gentleman to be her bridegroom?

JULIET
Not proud, you have; but thankful, that you have:
Proud can I never be of what I hate;
But thankful even for hate, that is meant love.

CAPULET
How now, how now, chop-logic! What is this?
'Proud,' and 'I thank you,' and 'I thank you not;'

And yet 'not proud,' mistress minion, you,

It will be Romeo, who you know I hate,
Rather than Paris. Now that's news!

LADY CAPULET
Here comes your dad; you tell him,
And see how he takes the news.

Enter CAPULET and Nurse

CAPULET
When the sun goes down, the mist falls;
But when Tybalt died
It poured with rain.
What are you girl? A fountain? Still crying?
In one little body
You are like a ship at sea in the wind;
For your eyes are the sea,
Flowing with tears; your body the ship,
Sailing in the salty flood of tears; your
sighs are the winds who rage with your
tears,
If you don't calm down, you'll wreck
Your whole storm tossed body. How is it
wife?
Have you told her our decision?

LADY CAPULET
Yes, but she isn't interested. She says to
thank you.
I wish she was dead.

CAPULET
Wait! Explain this to me, wife.
She refuses? Is she not grateful to us?
Is she not proud that such a man wants
her?
Unworthy as she is, that we have managed
to get such an amazing man to be her
husband?

JULIET
Not proud, but thankful for your efforts:
I can never be proud of what I hate;
But grateful because you meant it in love.

CAPULET
What is this riddle?
'Proud' and 'I thank you,' and 'I thank you
not;'
And yet 'not proud', you spoilt little brat,
you

Thank me no thankings, nor, proud me no prouds,
But fettle your fine joints 'gainst Thursday next,
To go with Paris to Saint Peter's Church,
Or I will drag thee on a hurdle thither.
Out, you green-sickness carrion! out, you baggage!
You tallow-face!

LADY CAPULET
Fie, fie! what, are you mad?

JULIET
Good father, I beseech you on my knees,
Hear me with patience but to speak a word.

CAPULET
Hang thee, young baggage! disobedient wretch!

I tell thee what: get thee to church o' Thursday,

Or never after look me in the face:
Speak not, reply not, do not answer me;
My fingers itch. Wife, we scarce thought us blest

That God had lent us but this only child;
But now I see this one is one too much,
And that we have a curse in having her:
Out on her, hilding!

Nurse
God in heaven bless her!
You are to blame, my lord, to rate her so.

CAPULET
And why, my lady wisdom? hold your tongue,
Good prudence; smatter with your gossips, go.

Nurse
I speak no treason.

CAPULET
O, God ye god-den.

Nurse
May not one speak?

CAPULET
Peace, you mumbling fool!
Utter your gravity o'er a gossip's bowl;
For here we need it not.

Don't thank me or be proud
But get yourself to next Thursday,
To Church with Paris,
Or I will drag you there as a traitor.
Get out, you lifeless corpse! You burden!
You pale face!

LADY CAPULET
Are you mad?

JULIET
Dad, I beg you on my knees,
Listen to me patiently.

CAPULET
You worthless burden! You disobedient
wretch!
I tell you what: get you to Church on
Thursday,
Or never again look at me:
Don't speak, don't say anything;
I want to slap you. Wife, we thought we
were lucky
To be given this one child;
But now I can see just one is too much,
And it is a curse of us to have her:
She disgusts me!

Nurse
God in heaven bless her!
You are wrong, Capulet, to treat her like
this.

CAPULET
And why, wise woman? Shut up,
Go chatter with the gossips.

Nurse
I don't have something bad to say.

CAPULET
For God's sake.

Nurse
Can I not speak?

CAPULET
Quiet, you mumbling fool!
Go and share your wisdom with gossips;
Here it is not needed.

LADY CAPULET

You are too hot.

CAPULET

God's bread! it makes me mad:
Day, night, hour, tide, time, work, play,
Alone, in company, still my care hath been
To have her match'd: and having now provided

A gentleman of noble parentage,
Of fair demesnes, youthful, and nobly train'd,
Stuff'd, as they say, with honourable parts,
Proportion'd as one's thought would wish a man;
And then to have a wretched puling fool,
A whining mammet, in her fortune's tender,
To answer 'I'll not wed; I cannot love,
I am too young; I pray you, pardon me.'
But, as you will not wed, I'll pardon you:
Graze where you will you shall not house with me:

Look to't, think on't, I do not use to jest.
Thursday is near; lay hand on heart, advise:
An you be mine, I'll give you to my friend;

And you be not, hang, beg, starve, die in
the streets,
For, by my soul, I'll ne'er acknowledge thee,

Nor what is mine shall never do thee good:
Trust to't, bethink you; I'll not be forsworn.

Exit

JULIET

Is there no pity sitting in the clouds,
That sees into the bottom of my grief?
O, sweet my mother, cast me not away!
Delay this marriage for a month, a week;
Or, if you do not, make the bridal bed
In that dim monument where Tybalt lies.

LADY CAPULET

Talk not to me, for I'll not speak a word:
Do as thou wilt, for I have done with thee.

Exit

JULIET

O God!--O nurse, how shall this be prevented?

LADY CAPULET

You are too wound up.

CAPULET

It makes me mad:
All this time
My aim has been
To get her married, and having now
Provided
a man who comes from a good family,
Good looking and intelligent,
Full of good qualities,
Everything you could wish for in a man;
And then to have foolish Juliet,
Crying, looking at her good luck,
Answering "I'll not marry; I cannot love.
I am too young; please forgive me.'
If you will not marry, I'll forgive you:
Eat where you want but it shall not be in
this house:
Think about it, I am not joking.
Thursday is close, Listen to my advice;
If you are mine, I will give you to my
friend,
If you are not mine, then hang, beg, starve
and die in the streets,
I promise, I will have nothing to do with
you,
Anything of mine will never do you good:
This about it, I will not break this promise.

Exit

JULIET

Can pity not
See how sad I am?
Oh mum, don't abandon me!
Delay the marriage for a month, a week;
Or, if you don't, make the wedding bed
In the same tomb where Tybalt lies.

LADY CAPULET

Don't talk to me, for I will not talk to you:
Do what you like, I am done with you.

Exit

JULIET

Oh God! Nurse, how shall this marriage to
Paris be stopped?

My husband is on earth, my faith in heaven;	I have a husband already, and my vows are holy;
How shall that faith return again to earth,	How can I bring my holy promises back to earth,
Unless that husband send it me from heaven	Unless my husband dies and releases me to love another?
By leaving earth? comfort me, counsel me.	Help me, tell me what to do.
Alack, alack, that heaven should practise stratagems	Why does heaven play tricks
Upon so soft a subject as myself!	On someone so weak as me!
What say'st thou? hast thou not a word of joy?	What do you say? Have you nothing good to say?
Some comfort, nurse.	Help me nurse.
Nurse	**Nurse**
Faith, here it is.	OK, here it is.
Romeo is banish'd; and all the world to nothing,	Romeo is banished; and
That he dares ne'er come back to challenge you;	He cannot come back here for you;
Or, if he do, it needs must be by stealth.	Or if he does, it must be by sneaking in.
Then, since the case so stands as now it doth,	Then, since this is the situation,
I think it best you married with the county.	I think you should marry Paris.
O, he's a lovely gentleman!	He's a lovely chap!
Romeo's a dishclout to him: an eagle, madam,	Romeo is nothing compared to him,
Hath not so green, so quick, so fair an eye	He's not as good looking as
As Paris hath. Beshrew my very heart,	Paris is. Curse my heart,
I think you are happy in this second match,	But I think this second marriage will make you happy,
For it excels your first: or if it did not,	As it is better than the one with Romeo
Your first is dead; or 'twere as good he were,	Romeo is dead, or as good as,
As living here and you no use of him.	Romeo doesn't live here so you get no use out of him.
JULIET	**JULIET**
Speakest thou from thy heart?	Are you speaking from your heart?
Nurse	**Nurse**
And from my soul too;	And my soul too;
Or else beshrew them both.	Or else curse them both.
JULIET	**JULIET**
Amen!	I agree!
Nurse	**Nurse**
What?	What?
JULIET	**JULIET**
Well, thou hast comforted me marvellous much.	Well you have comforted me really well
Go in: and tell my lady I am gone,	Go on, tell my mum I am going,
Having displeased my father, to Laurence' cell,	Having upset my dad, to Friar Laurence,
To make confession and to be absolved.	To make a confession and be forgiven.

Nurse	**Nurse**
Marry, I will; and this is wisely done.	OK I will; it's the best thing to do.
Exit	*Exit*
JULIET	**JULIET**
Ancient damnation! O most wicked fiend!	Damned old lady! Evil thing!
Is it more sin to wish me thus forsworn,	Is it worse that she wants me to cheat on Romeo,
Or to dispraise my lord with that same tongue	Or that she criticises him with the same tongue
Which she hath praised him with above compare	Which said such good things about him before?
So many thousand times? Go, counsellor;	Go , nurse;
Thou and my bosom henceforth shall be twain.	You shall never again know what is in my heart.
I'll to the friar, to know his remedy:	I will go the friar, hear his advice:
If all else fail, myself have power to die.	If all else fails I can always kill myself.
Exit	*Exit*

Act 4 Scene 1

ORIGINAL TEXT	MODERN TRANSLATION
Friar Laurence's cell.	Friar Laurence's place
Enter FRIAR LAURENCE and PARIS	*Enter FRIAR LAURENCE and PARIS*
FRIAR LAURENCE On Thursday, sir? the time is very short.	**FRIAR LAURENCE** On Thursday? That's very soon.
PARIS My father Capulet will have it so; And I am nothing slow to slack his haste.	**PARIS** Lord Capulet wants it that way; I have no reason to slow it down.
FRIAR LAURENCE You say you do not know the lady's mind: Uneven is the course, I like it not.	**FRIAR LAURENCE** You say you don't know Juliet's opinion: This is not fair, I don't like it.
PARIS Immoderately she weeps for Tybalt's death, And therefore have I little talk'd of love; For Venus smiles not in a house of tears. Now, sir, her father counts it dangerous That she doth give her sorrow so much sway, And in his wisdom hastes our marriage, To stop the inundation of her tears; Which, too much minded by herself alone, May be put from her by society: Now do you know the reason of this haste.	**PARIS** She is over sad about Tybalt's death, So I haven't talked much about love with her; Romance doesn't happen in places of grieving. Now, Lord Capulet thinks it is dangerous That she is so sad, And he thinks it a good idea for us to marry, To stop her crying; Which happens always when she is alone, May stop when she is not alone: Now you know why we hurry.
FRIAR LAURENCE [Aside] I would I knew not why it should be slow'd. Look, sir, here comes the lady towards my cell.	**FRIAR LAURENCE** (quietly) I wish I didn't know why it needs to be slowed down. Look, here comes Juliet now.
Enter JULIET	*Enter JULIET*
PARIS Happily met, my lady and my wife!	**PARIS** Good to see you my wife!
JULIET That may be, sir, when I may be a wife.	**JULIET** That may be the case, after we are married.

PARIS
That may be must be, love, on Thursday next.

JULIET
What must be shall be.

FRIAR LAURENCE
That's a certain text.

PARIS
Come you to make confession to this father?

JULIET
To answer that, I should confess to you.

PARIS
Do not deny to him that you love me.

JULIET
I will confess to you that I love him.

PARIS
So will ye, I am sure, that you love me.

JULIET
If I do so, it will be of more price,
Being spoke behind your back, than to your face.

PARIS
Poor soul, thy face is much abused with tears.

JULIET
The tears have got small victory by that;
For it was bad enough before their spite.

PARIS
Thou wrong'st it, more than tears, with that report.

JULIET
That is no slander, sir, which is a truth;
And what I spake, I spake it to my face.

PARIS
Thy face is mine, and thou hast slander'd it.

JULIET
It may be so, for it is not mine own.

PARIS
Not may be but must be, next Thursday.

JULIET
What must happen shall happen.

FRIAR LAURENCE
That's the truth.

PARIS
Have you come to confess to the friar?

JULIET
If I answer you, I will be confessing to you.

PARIS
Don't lie to him and say you don't love me.

JULIET
I will confess to you that I love him.

PARIS
I am sure you love me.

JULIET
If I do love you, it will be better,
For me to say it behind your back than to
your face.

PARIS
Poor thing, your face has been ruined with
tears.

JULIET
The tears aren't the ones that did that;
My face was ruined enough before I cried.

PARIS
You aren't right.

JULIET
I am telling the truth;
And I am telling it to my face.

PARIS
Your face belongs to me, and you have
criticised it.

JULIET
That may be true, for my face is not my
own.

Are you at leisure, holy father, now;
Or shall I come to you at evening mass?

FRIAR LAURENCE
My leisure serves me, pensive daughter, now.
My lord, we must entreat the time alone.

PARIS
God shield I should disturb devotion!

Juliet, on Thursday early will I rouse ye:
Till then, adieu; and keep this holy kiss.

Exit

JULIET
O shut the door! and when thou hast done so,

Come weep with me; past hope, past cure, past help!

FRIAR LAURENCE
Ah, Juliet, I already know thy grief;
It strains me past the compass of my wits:
I hear thou must, and nothing may prorogue it,
On Thursday next be married to this county.

JULIET
Tell me not, friar, that thou hear'st of this,
Unless thou tell me how I may prevent it:

If, in thy wisdom, thou canst give no help,
Do thou but call my resolution wise,
And with this knife I'll help it presently.
God join'd my heart and Romeo's, thou our hands;

And ere this hand, by thee to Romeo seal'd,

Shall be the label to another deed,
Or my true heart with treacherous revolt
Turn to another, this shall slay them both:

Therefore, out of thy long-experienced time,
Give me some present counsel, or, behold,
'Twixt my extremes and me this bloody knife
Shall play the umpire, arbitrating that
Which the commission of thy years and art
Could to no issue of true honour bring.
Be not so long to speak; I long to die,
If what thou speak'st speak not of remedy.

Are you free, friar, now;
Or shall I come tonight?

FRIAR LAURENCE
I am free to see you now.
Paris, I need to see Juliet alone.

PARIS
I wouldn't want to get in the way of such religious devotion!
Juliet, I will wake you on Thursday:
Until then goodbye, and take this kiss.

Exit

JULIET
Oh shut the door! And when you've done that
Come cry with me; this situation is hopeless and helpless!

FRIAR LAURENCE
Oh, Juliet, I know why you are upset;
It is driving me crazy too:
I hear you must, and nothing can delay it,
marry Paris next Thursday.

JULIET
Don't tell me, that you know about this,
Unless you also tell me how to stop it happening:
If, in your wisdom, you can't help me,
Just tell me my plan isn't stupid,
And with this knife I'll kill myself.
God joined my heart to Romeo's, you joined our hands;
And now this hand, which belongs to Romeo,
Shall be given to another man,
Or if Romeo cheated
and had another woman, this will kill them both:
You are clever and experienced,
Give me some advice, or watch,
As this bloody knife
Shall be the judge, resolving the thing
That your long years of experience
Cannot seem to solve.
Don't say nothing; I long to die,
If you cannot find a solution.

FRIAR LAURENCE

Hold, daughter: I do spy a kind of hope,
Which craves as desperate an execution.
As that is desperate which we would prevent.

If, rather than to marry County Paris,
Thou hast the strength of will to slay thyself,
Then is it likely thou wilt undertake
A thing like death to chide away this shame,

That copest with death himself to scape from it:

And, if thou darest, I'll give thee remedy.

JULIET

O, bid me leap, rather than marry Paris,

From off the battlements of yonder tower;
Or walk in thievish ways; or bid me lurk
Where serpents are; chain me with roaring bears;
Or shut me nightly in a charnel-house,
O'er-cover'd quite with dead men's rattling bones,
With reeky shanks and yellow chapless skulls;
Or bid me go into a new-made grave
And hide me with a dead man in his shroud;
Things that, to hear them told, have made me tremble;
And I will do it without fear or doubt,
To live an unstain'd wife to my sweet love.

FRIAR LAURENCE

Hold, then; go home, be merry, give consent
To marry Paris: Wednesday is to-morrow:
To-morrow night look that thou lie alone;
Let not thy nurse lie with thee in thy chamber:
Take thou this vial, being then in bed,
And this distilled liquor drink thou off;
When presently through all thy veins shall run
A cold and drowsy humour, for no pulse
Shall keep his native progress, but surcease:
No warmth, no breath, shall testify thou livest;

The roses in thy lips and cheeks shall fade
To paly ashes, thy eyes' windows fall,
Like death, when he shuts up the day of life;
Each part, deprived of supple government,

Shall, stiff and stark and cold, appear like death:

And in this borrow'd likeness of shrunk death

FRIAR LAURENCE

Wait: I do see a small glimmer of hope,
Which is a huge risk to take.
As desperate as what we are trying to stop.
If, rather than marry Paris,
You would kill yourself,
Then you will probably accept
A thing like death to get rid of this problem.
You can fight with death to escape the situation:
And, if you're brave enough to do it, I will give you the solution.

JULIET

Oh, ask me to jump, rather than marry Paris,
From the top of that high tower;
Or walk through streets full of criminals; or sit with snakes; chain me to roaring bears;
Or shut me up each night in a morgue,
Covered with dead men's bones,
Stinking flesh and jawless skulls;
Or ask me to climb into a newly dug grave
And hide me with the body of a dead man;
These things, just to hear them, scare me;

But I will do them unafraid,
To live with Romeo.

FRIAR LAURENCE

Wait then; go home, be happy, agree
To marry Paris: tomorrow is Wednesday:
Tomorrow night sleep on your own;
Don't let the nurse sleep in your room:
Take this bottle, when in bed,
And drink the potion inside it;
The potion will run through your veins
And make you appear to be dead
Your pulse will stop:
You will be cold, not breathing, appearing dead;
The colour shall fade from your face
To paleness. Your eyes will close
Like you are dead.
Each part of you, with nothing controlling it,
Shall go stiff and cold, appearing like death:
And looking like you are dead

Thou shalt continue two and forty hours,	You will stay for 42 hours,
And then awake as from a pleasant sleep.	And then wake up like from a nice sleep.
Now, when the bridegroom in the morning comes	So, when Paris comes
To rouse thee from thy bed, there art thou dead:	To wake you up, there you are dead:
Then, as the manner of our country is,	Then, as they do in our country,
In thy best robes uncover'd on the bier	They will dress you up, put you in an open coffin
Thou shalt be borne to that same ancient vault	And take you to the ancient tomb
Where all the kindred of the Capulets lie.	Where all your relatives lie.
In the mean time, against thou shalt awake,	Whilst this is happening, before you wake up,
Shall Romeo by my letters know our drift,	I will write to Romeo and tell him about it,
And hither shall he come: and he and I	And he shall come here: and he and I
Will watch thy waking, and that very night	Will watch you wake up, and that night
Shall Romeo bear thee hence to Mantua.	Romeo will take to Mantua.
And this shall free thee from this present shame;	And that will free you from your current problem;
If no inconstant toy, nor womanish fear,	If womanly fear,
Abate thy valour in the acting it.	Doesn't stop your bravery.
JULIET	**JULIET**
Give me, give me! O, tell not me of fear!	Give it to me, give it to me! Don't tell me about fear.
FRIAR LAURENCE	**FRIAR LAURENCE**
Hold; get you gone, be strong and prosperous	Go now, be strong and successful
In this resolve: I'll send a friar with speed	In this decision: I'll send a priest quickly
To Mantua, with my letters to thy lord.	To Mantua, with letters to Romeo.
JULIET	**JULIET**
Love give me strength! and strength shall help afford.	God make me strong! and strength will help me do it.
Farewell, dear father!	Goodbye, father!
Exeunt	*Exit*

Act 4 Scene 2

ORIGINAL TEXT	MODERN TRANSLATION
Hall in Capulet's house.	Hall in Capulet's house.
Enter CAPULET, LADY CAPULET, Nurse, and two Servingmen	*Enter CAPULET, LADY CAPULET, Nurse and two servants.*
CAPULET So many guests invite as here are writ.	**CAPULET** Invite the guests written here.
Exit First Servant	*Exit First Servant*
Sirrah, go hire me twenty cunning cooks.	Go and hire me twenty good cooks
Second Servant You shall have none ill, sir; for I'll try if they can lick their fingers.	**Second Servant** You shall have no bad cooks; I'll test them by making them lick their fingers.
CAPULET How canst thou try them so?	**CAPULET** How can you test them like that?
Second Servant Marry, sir, 'tis an ill cook that cannot lick his own fingers: therefore he that cannot lick his fingers goes not with me.	**Second Servant** A bad cook cannot lick his fingers: so anyone who cannot lick his fingers will not be hired.
CAPULET Go, be gone.	**CAPULET** Go, go away.
Exit Second Servant	*Exit Second Servant*
We shall be much unfurnished for this time. What, is my daughter gone to Friar Laurence?	We will be unprepared for this wedding. Has Juliet gone to the Friar?
Nurse Ay, forsooth.	**Nurse** Yes, that's true.
CAPULET Well, he may chance to do some good on her: A peevish self-will'd harlotry it is.	**CAPULET** Well, he may do some good to her: A stubborn girl she is.
Nurse See where she comes from shrift with merry look.	**Nurse** Here she comes now, looking happy.
Enter JULIET	*Enter JULIET*
CAPULET How now, my headstrong! where have you been gadding?	**CAPULET** My headstrong daughter! Where have you been?

JULIET
Where I have learn'd me to repent the sin

Of disobedient opposition
To you and your behests, and am enjoin'd
By holy Laurence to fall prostrate here,
And beg your pardon: pardon, I beseech you!

Henceforward I am ever ruled by you.

CAPULET
Send for the county; go tell him of this:
I'll have this knot knit up to-morrow morning.

JULIET
I met the youthful lord at Laurence' cell;
And gave him what becomed love I might,
Not step o'er the bounds of modesty.

CAPULET
Why, I am glad on't; this is well: stand up:
This is as't should be. Let me see the county;
Ay, marry, go, I say, and fetch him hither.
Now, afore God! this reverend holy friar,
Our whole city is much bound to him.

JULIET
Nurse, will you go with me into my closet,
To help me sort such needful ornaments
As you think fit to furnish me to-morrow?

LADY CAPULET
No, not till Thursday; there is time enough.

CAPULET
Go, nurse, go with her: we'll to church to-morrow.

Exeunt JULIET and Nurse

LADY CAPULET
We shall be short in our provision:
'Tis now near night.

CAPULET
Tush, I will stir about,
And all things shall be well, I warrant thee, wife:

JULIET
Where I have learned to turn from my wrongdoing
of not obeying you
and what you tell me to do, and I am told
by Friar Laurence to fall before you,
And beg you forgive me: please do forgive me!
From now on I will do what you say.

CAPULET
Send for Paris; tell him about this:
I will make this wedding happen tomorrow morning.

JULIET
I met Paris at Friar Laurence's
And treated him with love,
Just as much as I should do without appearing over flirty.

CAPULET
I am glad, this is good: stand up:
This is how it should be. Let me see Paris;
Yes, go and get him, bring him here.
Now, I tell you, Friar Laurence,
We all owe him a lot.

JULIET
Nurse, will you come with me to my closet,
To help me pick out the jewellery
You think I should wear tomorrow.

LADY CAPULET
No, not til Thursday; there is plenty of time.

CAPULET
Go on nurse, go with her: the wedding will take place tomorrow.

Exit JULIET and Nurse

LADY CAPULET
We haven't got enough supplies:
It's nearly night time.

CAPULET
I will sort things out,
Everything will be fine, I promise you:

Go thou to Juliet, help to deck up her; I'll not to bed to-night; let me alone; I'll play the housewife for this once. What, ho! They are all forth. Well, I will walk myself To County Paris, to prepare him up Against to-morrow: my heart is wondrous light, Since this same wayward girl is so reclaim'd. *Exeunt*	Go to Juliet, help to dress her up; I'll not go to bed tonight; leave me alone; I'll be the housewife for one. They are all gone. Well, I will walk alone To Paris, to prepare him for Tomorrow: I feel so happy, Now Juliet is behaving herself again. *Exit*

Act 4 Scene 3

ORIGINAL TEXT	MODERN TRANSLATION
Juliet's chamber.	Juliet's room.
Enter JULIET and Nurse	*Enter JULIET and Nurse*
JULIET Ay, those attires are best: but, gentle nurse, I pray thee, leave me to my self to-night, For I have need of many orisons To move the heavens to smile upon my state, Which, well thou know'st, is cross, and full of sin.	**JULIET** Those clothes are best, but nurse, Please leave me alone tonight, I have lots of prayers to pray To make heaven happy with me, You know I have done so much wrong.
Enter LADY CAPULET	*Enter LADY CAPULET*
LADY CAPULET What, are you busy, ho? need you my help?	**LADY CAPULET** Are you busy? Do you need my help?
JULIET No, madam; we have cull'd such necessaries As are behoveful for our state to-morrow: So please you, let me now be left alone, And let the nurse this night sit up with you; For, I am sure, you have your hands full all, In this so sudden business.	**JULIET** No; we have worked out the best things For me to wear tomorrow: So please leave me alone, And let the nurse stay with you tonight; For I am sure you have lots to do, For this sudden wedding.
LADY CAPULET Good night: Get thee to bed, and rest; for thou hast need.	**LADY CAPULET** Good night: Get to bed and sleep; you need to rest.
Exeunt LADY CAPULET and Nurse	*Exit LADY CAPULET and Nurse*
JULIET Farewell! God knows when we shall meet again. I have a faint cold fear thrills through my veins, That almost freezes up the heat of life: I'll call them back again to comfort me: Nurse! What should she do here? My dismal scene I needs must act alone. Come, vial. What if this mixture do not work at all? Shall I be married then to-morrow morning? No, no: this shall forbid it: lie thou there.	**JULIET** Goodbye! God knows when we shall meet again. I am so afraid, It almost kills me: I'll call them back to calm me down: Nurse! What good would she do? I need to do this alone. Come, bottle. What if the poison doesn't work? Shall I then be married tomorrow morning? No, no: I won't let it happen: you wait there.
Laying down her dagger	*Laying down her knife*

130

What if it be a poison, which the friar Subtly hath minister'd to have me dead, Lest in this marriage he should be dishonour'd, Because he married me before to Romeo? I fear it is: and yet, methinks, it should not, For he hath still been tried a holy man. How if, when I am laid into the tomb, I wake before the time that Romeo Come to redeem me? there's a fearful point! Shall I not, then, be stifled in the vault, To whose foul mouth no healthsome air breathes in, And there die strangled ere my Romeo comes? Or, if I live, is it not very like, The horrible conceit of death and night, Together with the terror of the place,-- As in a vault, an ancient receptacle, Where, for these many hundred years, the bones Of all my buried ancestors are packed: Where bloody Tybalt, yet but green in earth, Lies festering in his shroud; where, as they say, At some hours in the night spirits resort;-- Alack, alack, is it not like that I, So early waking, what with loathsome smells, And shrieks like mandrakes' torn out of the earth, That living mortals, hearing them, run mad:-- O, if I wake, shall I not be distraught, Environed with all these hideous fears? And madly play with my forefather's joints? And pluck the mangled Tybalt from his shroud? And, in this rage, with some great kinsman's bone, As with a club, dash out my desperate brains? O, look! methinks I see my cousin's ghost Seeking out Romeo, that did spit his body Upon a rapier's point: stay, Tybalt, stay! Romeo, I come! this do I drink to thee. *She falls upon her bed, within the curtains*	What if this is a fatal poison, that the friar Is giving me to kill me, So he won't get in trouble himself, Because he's already married me to Romeo? I am afraid it is, but it cannot be, Because he is a holy man. What if, when I am laid in the tomb, I wake up before Romeo Comes to save me. That's a scary point! Won't I still be locked in the vault, Where there is no fresh air to breathe, And there die of suffocation before Romeo comes? Or, if I live, it's not nice The darkness of night, In that scary place... A vault where, For hundreds of years, the bones Of all my dead ancestors are stuffed: Where Tybalt, only recently died, Lies rotting in his grave clothes; where, as the saying goes, Spirits of the dead are... Oh no, oh no, is it like that? Waking early, with awful smells, And ghosts screaming. The sound of which scares living people, Oh, if I wake, won't I be scared witless, Surrounded by these scary things? Go mad and play with the bones of the dead? Pull Tybalt out of his grave clothes? And in anger, with some relative's bone Like a bat, bash my own head in? Oh look! I think I see Tybalt's ghost Looking for Romeo that killed him With a sword: wait Tybalt, wait! Romeo, I am coming! I drink this to you. *She falls upon her bed.*

Act 4 Scene 4

ORIGINAL TEXT	MODERN TRANSLATION
Hall in Capulet's house.	Capulet's house.
Enter LADY CAPULET and Nurse	*Enter LADY CAPULET and Nurse*
LADY CAPULET Hold, take these keys, and fetch more spices, nurse.	**LADY CAPULET** Take these keys, and get more spices, nurse.
Nurse They call for dates and quinces in the pastry.	**Nurse** The pastry kitchen is asking for dates and quince.
Enter CAPULET	*Enter CAPULET*
CAPULET Come, stir, stir, stir! the second cock hath crow'd, The curfew-bell hath rung, 'tis three o'clock: Look to the baked meats, good Angelica: Spare not for the cost.	**CAPULET** Come on, wake, wake wake! The second cock has crow'd, The curfew bell has rung - it's three o'clock: Go and get baked meat, Angelica: Buy the best there is.
Nurse Go, you cot-quean, go, Get you to bed; faith, You'll be sick to-morrow For this night's watching.	**Nurse** Go, you old housewife, go Go to bed, else you will be sick tomorrow For staying up all night tonight.
CAPULET No, not a whit: what! I have watch'd ere now All night for lesser cause, and ne'er been sick.	**CAPULET** No, not a chance. I have been up all night before for much less reason and never got been sick from it.
LADY CAPULET Ay, you have been a mouse-hunt in your time; But I will watch you from such watching now.	**LADY CAPULET** Yes, you've had women in your time; But I will make sure you don't stay up too late.
Exeunt LADY CAPULET and Nurse	*Exit LADY CAPULET and Nurse*
CAPULET A jealous hood, a jealous hood!	**CAPULET** What a jealous woman!
Enter three or four Servingmen, with spits, logs, and baskets	*Enter three or four servants with spits, logs and baskets*
Now, fellow,	Now, man,

What's there?	What have you got there?
First Servant Things for the cook, sir; but I know not what.	**First Servant** Things for the cook, but I don't know what.
CAPULET Make haste, make haste.	**CAPULET** Hurry up, hurry up.
Exit First Servant	*Exit first servant*
Sirrah, fetch drier logs: Call Peter, he will show thee where they are.	Get drier logs: Call Peter, he will show you where they are.
Second Servant I have a head, sir, that will find out logs, And never trouble Peter for the matter.	**Second Servant** I can find them myself sir, And not need to bother Peter.
Exit	*Exit*
CAPULET Mass, and well said; a merry whoreson, ha! Thou shalt be logger-head. Good faith, 'tis day: The county will be here with music straight, For so he said he would: I hear him near.	**CAPULET** Well said: a funny guy, ha! His head is full of logs. Oh my, it's morning: Paris will be here with music soon, As he said he would: I can hear him nearby.
Music within	*Music plays*
Nurse! Wife! What, ho! What, nurse, I say!	Nurse! Wife! Nurse!
Re-enter Nurse	*Re-enter Nurse*
Go waken Juliet, go and trim her up; I'll go and chat with Paris: hie, make haste, Make haste; the bridegroom he is come already: Make haste, I say.	Go and wake Juliet, get her ready; I'll go and speak to Paris: hurry up, Hurry up; Paris is here already: Hurry up, I say.
Exeunt	*Exit*

Act 4 Scene 5

ORIGINAL TEXT	MODERN TRANSLATION
Juliet's chamber.	Juliet's room.
Enter Nurse	*Enter Nurse*
Nurse Mistress! what, mistress! Juliet! fast, I warrant her, she: Why, lamb! why, lady! fie, you slug-a-bed! Why, love, I say! madam! sweet-heart! why, bride!	**Nurse** Mistress! Hey, mistress! Juliet! Fast asleep I bet: Lady! You lazy bones! Love, I say! Madam! Sweet-heart! Bride!
What, not a word? you take your pennyworths now;	What, not saying anything? You get your beauty sleep now;
Sleep for a week; for the next night, I warrant,	Sleep as much as you can, for tomorrow, I bet,
The County Paris hath set up his rest, That you shall rest but little. God forgive me, Marry, and amen, how sound is she asleep! I must needs wake her. Madam, madam, madam!	Paris has had his rest And won't let you rest at all. How deeply she is asleep! I need to wake her up. Madam, madam, madam!
Ay, let the county take you in your bed; He'll fright you up, i' faith. Will it not be?	Let Paris get into your bed; He'll wake you up, I bet. Won't he?
Undraws the curtains	*Opens the curtains*
What, dress'd! and in your clothes! and down again!	What, you're dressed in your clothes! But back asleep!
I must needs wake you; Lady! lady! lady! Alas, alas! Help, help! my lady's dead! O, well-a-day, that ever I was born! Some aqua vitae, ho! My lord! my lady!	I must wake you up; Lady! lady! lady! Oh no, oh no! Help, help! Juliet is dead! Oh curse the day I was ever born! Get me some alcohol! Lord and lady Capulet!
Enter LADY CAPULET	*Enter LADY CAPULET*
LADY CAPULET What noise is here?	**LADY CAPULET** What noise is this?
Nurse O lamentable day!	**Nurse** Oh terrible day!
LADY CAPULET What is the matter?	**LADY CAPULET** What's the matter?
Nurse Look, look! O heavy day!	**Nurse** Look, look! Oh awful day!

LADY CAPULET

O me, O me! My child, my only life,

Revive, look up, or I will die with thee!

Help, help! Call help.

Enter CAPULET

CAPULET

For shame, bring Juliet forth; her lord is come.

Nurse

She's dead, deceased, she's dead; alack the day!

LADY CAPULET

Alack the day, she's dead, she's dead, she's dead!

CAPULET

Ha! let me see her: out, alas! she's cold:
Her blood is settled, and her joints are stiff;

Life and these lips have long been separated:
Death lies on her like an untimely frost
Upon the sweetest flower of all the field.

Nurse

O lamentable day!

LADY CAPULET

O woful time!

CAPULET

Death, that hath ta'en her hence to make me wail,

Ties up my tongue, and will not let me speak.

Enter FRIAR LAURENCE and PARIS, with Musicians

FRIAR LAURENCE

Come, is the bride ready to go to church?

CAPULET

Ready to go, but never to return.

O son! the night before thy wedding-day
Hath Death lain with thy wife. There she lies,
Flower as she was, deflowered by him.
Death is my son-in-law, Death is my heir;

LADY CAPULET

Oh my, oh my! My child, my reason for living,
Wake up, come to live or I will die with you!
Help, help! Call for help.

Enter CAPULET

CAPULET

Bring Juliet out; her husband is here.

Nurse

She's dead, dead, dead; curse this day!

LADY CAPULET

Curse this day, she's dead, she's dead, she's dead!

CAPULET

Let me see her: she's cold:
Her blood has stopped pumping, her joints stiff;
Life has gone from her lips:
Death lies on her like frost out of season
Upon the sweetest flower in the field.

Nurse

Oh awful day!

LADY CAPULET

Oh terrible time!

CAPULET

Death, that has taken her, does make me cry,
It ties up my tongue, I cannot speak.

Enter FRIAR LAURENCE and PARIS, with Musicians

FRIAR LAURENCE

Is the bride ready to go to Church?

CAPULET

Ready to go to Church but never come back.
Oh Paris! The night before your wedding
Death has taken Juliet. There she lies,
Flower that she was, deflowered by Death.
Death is now my son-in-law and heir;

My daughter he hath wedded: I will die,
And leave him all; life, living, all is Death's.

PARIS
Have I thought long to see this morning's face,
And doth it give me such a sight as this?

LADY CAPULET
Accursed, unhappy, wretched, hateful day!
Most miserable hour that e'er time saw
In lasting labour of his pilgrimage!
But one, poor one, one poor and loving child,
But one thing to rejoice and solace in,
And cruel death hath catch'd it from my sight!

Nurse
O woe! O woful, woful, woful day!
Most lamentable day, most woful day,
That ever, ever, I did yet behold!
O day! O day! O day! O hateful day!
Never was seen so black a day as this:
O woful day, O woful day!

PARIS
Beguiled, divorced, wronged, spited, slain!

Most detestable death, by thee beguil'd,
By cruel cruel thee quite overthrown!
O love! O life! not life, but love in death!

CAPULET
Despised, distressed, hated, martyr'd, kill'd!
Uncomfortable time, why camest thou now
To murder, murder our solemnity?
O child! O child! my soul, and not my child!
Dead art thou! Alack! my child is dead;
And with my child my joys are buried.

FRIAR LAURENCE
Peace, ho, for shame! confusion's cure lives not

In these confusions. Heaven and yourself
Had part in this fair maid; now heaven hath all,
And all the better is it for the maid:
Your part in her you could not keep from death,

But heaven keeps his part in eternal life.

Juliet has married him: I will die,
And leave him everything I have.
Everything is Death's.

PARIS
Have I waited so long for this morning to come,
Only for it to end up like this?

LADY CAPULET
Cursed, unhappy, hateful day!
Most miserable hour that ever was
In all of time!
I had just one loving child,
And one thing to be happy about,
And death has taken it from me!

Nurse
Oh sadness! Oh sad, sad, sad day!
Most awful day, most terrible day,
That ever, ever, I did see!
Oh day! Oh day! Oh day! Oh hateful day!
Never was there such an evil day as this:
Oh terrible, terrible day!

PARIS
Juliet was tricked, wronged, divorced, and killed!
Most horrible death, you tricked her,
Cruel cruel death took her!
Oh love! Oh life! Life is over now my love is dead.

CAPULET
Hated, distressed, sacrificed, killed!
Why did this happen now at this time,
That you ruin this wedding day?
Oh child! Child! My soul, not my child!
You are dead! Juliet is dead;
And with her my happiness is buried.

FRIAR LAURENCE
Be quiet! The cure for confusion is not
to shout your heads off. Heaven gave
Juliet to you and now heaven has her back,
And that is better for Juliet:
You could not stop her from one day dying,
But in heaven she will live forever.

The most you sought was her promotion;	You wanted her to advance in life through marriage,
For 'twas your heaven she should be advanced:	That was what would make you happy:
And weep ye now, seeing she is advanced	And now you cry, seeing she has gone
Above the clouds, as high as heaven itself?	As high as heaven?
O, in this love, you love your child so ill,	Oh, you do Juliet no favours,
That you run mad, seeing that she is well:	Shouting your head off, considering she is well in heaven,
	Earthly marriage soon goes bad;
She's not well married that lives married long;	But it's best to marry you and die young.
But she's best married that dies married young.	Dry your eyes, stick your rosemary
Dry up your tears, and stick your rosemary	On this pretty corpse; and, as is the way,
On this fair corse; and, as the custom is,	Dress her at her best then carry her to Church:
In all her best array bear her to church:	for though it's normal to cry,
	We should be happy for her.
For though fond nature bids us an lament,	
Yet nature's tears are reason's merriment.	

CAPULET

All things that we ordained festival,	All the things we organised for the wedding,
	Can now be used for the funeral;
Turn from their office to black funeral;	Our instruments turn to sadness,
Our instruments to melancholy bells,	Our wedding food become funeral food,
Our wedding cheer to a sad burial feast,	Our celebratory songs to sad funeral songs,
Our solemn hymns to sullen dirges change,	Our wedding flowers be used for to cover the dead body;
Our bridal flowers serve for a buried corse,	And everything be used for the opposite of what was planned.
And all things change them to the contrary.	

FRIAR LAURENCE

Sir, go you in; and, madam, go with him;	Sir, you go in; and you madam go with him;
And go, Sir Paris; every one prepare	And you go too Paris, everyone prepare
To follow this fair corse unto her grave:	To take Juliet to her grave:
The heavens do lour upon you for some ill;	A curse of the gods is upon you for some sin;
Move them no more by crossing their high will.	Let's not aggravate them any more by going against their plan.

Exeunt CAPULET, LADY CAPULET, PARIS, and FRIAR LAURENCE	*Exit CAPULET, LADY CAPULET, PARIS and FRIAR LAURENCE*

First Musician

Faith, we may put up our pipes, and be gone.	We can put our instruments away and go home.

Nurse

Honest goodfellows, ah, put up, put up;	Good men, put them away, put them away;
For, well you know, this is a pitiful case.	For as you know this is an awful situation.

Exit	*Exit*
First Musician Ay, by my troth, the case may be amended.	**First Musician** Yes, things could be better.
Enter PETER	*Enter PETER*
PETER Musicians, O, musicians, 'Heart's ease, Heart's ease:' O, an you will have me live, play 'Heart's ease.'	**PETER** Musicians, play the tune 'Heart's Ease' Oh I will die if you don't play "Heart's ease.'
First Musician Why 'Heart's ease?'	**First Musician** Why that song?
PETER O, musicians, because my heart itself plays 'My heart is full of woe:' O, play me some merry dump, to comfort me.	**PETER** Oh musicians, because my heart is playing the song 'My Heart is Full of Sadness'. Play some happier sad tune to comfort me.
First Musician Not a dump we; 'tis no time to play now.	**First Musician** Not a sad song, it's not the time to play one.
PETER You will not, then?	**PETER** You won't do it then?
First Musician No.	**First Musician** No.
PETER I will then give it you soundly.	**PETER** Then I will give it to you.
First Musician What will you give us?	**First Musician** What will you give us?
PETER No money, on my faith, but the gleek; I will give you the minstrel.	**PETER** No money, I promise, but a trick; I will call you a minstrel.
First Musician Then I will give you the serving-creature.	**First Musician** Then I will give you a serving-creature.
PETER Then will I lay the serving-creature's dagger on your pate. I will carry no crotchets: I'll re you, I'll fa you; do you note me?	**PETER** Then I will hit you on the head with the serving-creature's dagger. I'll make you sing, do you hear me?

First Musician
An you re us and fa us, you note us.

Second Musician
Pray you, put up your dagger, and put out your wit.

PETER
Then have at you with my wit! I will dry-beat you with an iron wit, and put up my iron dagger. Answer me like men:
'When griping grief the heart doth wound,
And doleful dumps the mind oppress,
Then music with her silver sound'--
why 'silver sound'? why 'music with her silver sound'? What say you, Simon Catling?

Musician
Marry, sir, because silver hath a sweet sound.

PETER
Pretty! What say you, Hugh Rebeck?

Second Musician
I say 'silver sound,' because musicians sound for silver.

PETER
Pretty too! What say you, James Soundpost?

Third Musician
Faith, I know not what to say.

PETER
O, I cry you mercy; you are the singer: I will say

for you. It is 'music with her silver sound,' because musicians have no gold for sounding:

'Then music with her silver sound
With speedy help doth lend redress.'

Exit

First Musician
What a pestilent knave is this same!

First Musician
If you make us sing you will hear us.

Second Musician
Please, put away your sword and stop your banter.

PETER
Then I will attack you with my banter! I will hit you with my jokes, then pull out my knife. Answer me like men:
"When sadness takes over your heart,
And makes your mind depressed,
The music with her silver sound'
Why is it 'silver sound'? Why 'music with her silver sound?' What do you say? Simon Catling?

Musician
Well, because silver has a sweet sound.

PETER
That's a stupid answer. What do you say, Hugh Rebeck?

Second Musician
'Silver sound' because musicians make music for silver money.

PETER
Silly too! What do you say James Soundpost?

Third Musician
I don't know what to say.

PETER
Oh, I'm sorry; you are the singer; I will tell you
It is 'music with her silver sound,'
Because musicians have no gold to make sounds with:
'Then music with her silver sound
Makes you feel good'.

Exit

First Musician
What an annoying man this guy is!

Second Musician	**Second Musician**
Hang him, Jack! Come, we'll in here; tarry for the mourners, and stay dinner.	Forget him, Jack! Come on. We'll go in here, wait for the mourners and stay for dinner.
Exeunt	*Exit*

Second Musician

Hang him, Jack! Come, we'll in here; tarry for the mourners, and stay dinner.

Act 5 Scene 1

ORIGINAL TEXT	MODERN TRANSLATION
Mantua. A street.	A street in Mantua.
Enter ROMEO	*Enter ROMEO*
ROMEO If I may trust the flattering truth of sleep, My dreams presage some joyful news at hand: My bosom's lord sits lightly in his throne; And all this day an unaccustom'd spirit Lifts me above the ground with cheerful thoughts. I dreamt my lady came and found me dead-- Strange dream, that gives a dead man leave to think!-- And breathed such life with kisses in my lips, That I revived, and was an emperor. Ah me! how sweet is love itself possess'd, When but love's shadows are so rich in joy!	**ROMEO** If I can trust what goes on in sleep, My dreams tell me there is good news coming: My heart is ruled by love; And all day an odd feeling Has made me really happy. I dreamt that Juliet came and found me dead.. A dream that lets dead men think is weird! And she kissed me on my mouth, And brought my back to life. And once alive I was an emperor. Ah how great it is to have the one you live, When just thinking about them makes you so happy.
Enter BALTHASAR, booted	*BALTHASAR enters*
News from Verona!--How now, Balthasar! Dost thou not bring me letters from the friar? How doth my lady? Is my father well? How fares my Juliet? that I ask again; For nothing can be ill, if she be well.	It must be news from Verona! What is it Balthasar! Do you not have letters for me from the Friar? How is Juliet? Is my dad OK? How is Juliet doing? I ask again; Nothing can be bad if she is OK.
BALTHASAR Then she is well, and nothing can be ill: Her body sleeps in Capel's monument, And her immortal part with angels lives. I saw her laid low in her kindred's vault, And presently took post to tell it you: O, pardon me for bringing these ill news, Since you did leave it for my office, sir.	**BALTHASAR** Then she is well, and everything is OK: She lies in the Capulet family tomb, And her soul is in heaven with the angels. I saw her dead body in the tomb, And then came to tell you: I am so sorry to bring such bad news, Since you made it my job to bring news.
ROMEO Is it even so? then I defy you, stars! Thou know'st my lodging: get me ink and paper, And hire post-horses; I will hence to-night.	**ROMEO** Is it true? I hate you, fate! If you want me, you know where I am: get me pen and paper, And hire me a horse to ride: I am leaving tonight to go to Verona.

BALTHASAR
I do beseech you, sir, have patience:
Your looks are pale and wild, and do import
Some misadventure.

ROMEO
Tush, thou art deceived:
Leave me, and do the thing I bid thee do.
Hast thou no letters to me from the friar?

BALTHASAR
No, my good lord.

ROMEO
No matter: get thee gone,
And hire those horses; I'll be with thee straight.

Exit BALTHASAR

Well, Juliet, I will lie with thee to-night.

Let's see for means: O mischief, thou art swift

To enter in the thoughts of desperate men!
I do remember an apothecary,--
And hereabouts he dwells,--which late I noted
In tatter'd weeds, with overwhelming brows,

Culling of simples; meagre were his looks,
Sharp misery had worn him to the bones:
And in his needy shop a tortoise hung,
An alligator stuff'd, and other skins
Of ill-shaped fishes; and about his shelves
A beggarly account of empty boxes,
Green earthen pots, bladders and musty seeds,
Remnants of packthread and old cakes of roses,
Were thinly scatter'd, to make up a show.

Noting this penury, to myself I said
'An if a man did need a poison now,
Whose sale is present death in Mantua,
Here lives a caitiff wretch would sell it him.'
O, this same thought did but forerun my need;

And this same needy man must sell it me.
As I remember, this should be the house.
Being holiday, the beggar's shop is shut.
What, ho! apothecary!

BALTHASAR
Please, Romeo, be patient:
You are mad and angry and about to
do something bad.

ROMEO
You are wrong:
Leave me alone, and do as I asked.
Have you not got any letters for me from
the friar?

BALTHASAR
No.

ROMEO
It doesn't matter. Go away,
hire me horses. I will be with you soon.

Exit BALTHASAR

Well, Juliet, I will be lying down with you
tonight.
Let's see how. Oh bad thoughts you are
quick
to enter the mind of desperate men!
I remember a medicine man..
And he lives around here I saw lately
He wore messy clothes, and had huge
eyebrows,
He looked poor,
And worn out from a tough life:
In his shop was hung a tortoise,
A stuffed alligator and other skins
Of odd shaped fish; and on his shelves
A few empty boxes,
Pots of clay and some seeds,
Some old string and crushed up rose petals
Were placed around, to make it look like
he had things in the shop.
Noticing this, I said to myself
'If a man needed some poison,
Which is illegal to sell in Mantua,
Here is a man who would sell it to him.'
This idea came into my head before I
needed it;
And this same man must sell it to me.
As far as I can remember, this is his house.
Being a holiday, his shop is closed.
Hey, medicine man!

Enter Apothecary	*Enter the pharmacist*
Apothecary Who calls so loud?	**Apothecary** Who is shouting?
ROMEO Come hither, man. I see that thou art poor: Hold, there is forty ducats: let me have A dram of poison, such soon-speeding gear As will disperse itself through all the veins That the life-weary taker may fall dead And that the trunk may be discharged of breath As violently as hasty powder fired Doth hurry from the fatal cannon's womb.	**ROMEO** Come here. I can see that you are poor: Here is some money: give me Some poison which works quickly And will quickly spread through my body And kill me. And take my breath away As quickly as gunpowder Explodes in a cannon.
Apothecary Such mortal drugs I have; but Mantua's law Is death to any he that utters them.	**Apothecary** I do have drugs like these, but the law of this City is that I will be killed if I give them.
ROMEO Art thou so bare and full of wretchedness, And fear'st to die? famine is in thy cheeks, Need and oppression starveth in thine eyes, Contempt and beggary hangs upon thy back; The world is not thy friend nor the world's law; The world affords no law to make thee rich; Then be not poor, but break it, and take this.	**ROMEO** Are you so weak, And afraid to die? You are clearly starving, It's clear you are in desperate need, You are poor and nearly a beggar; The world is not your friend and neither is the law; There is no law to make you rich; So don't be poor, break the law and take the money.
Apothecary My poverty, but not my will, consents.	**Apothecary** My need for money, more than my happiness to do this, means I will accept your offer.
ROMEO I pay thy poverty, and not thy will.	**ROMEO** I pay your poverty, not your choice.
Apothecary Put this in any liquid thing you will, And drink it off; and, if you had the strength Of twenty men, it would dispatch you straight.	**Apothecary** Put this in any liquid, And drink it; and even if you were as strong as twenty men, it would kill you right away.
ROMEO There is thy gold, worse poison to men's souls, Doing more murders in this loathsome world,	**ROMEO** Here is your money. Money has a worse effect on people than poison, Killing more people in this world,

Than these poor compounds that thou mayst not sell. I sell thee poison; thou hast sold me none. Farewell: buy food, and get thyself in flesh. Come, cordial and not poison, go with me To Juliet's grave; for there must I use thee. *Exeunt*	Than these poisons that you are not allowed to sell. The money I am giving you is the real poison; you haven't sold any to me. Goodbye: use the money to buy food, and yourself fed up a bit. Come, medicine not poison, come with me To Juliet's grave and I will use you there. *Exit*

ORIGINAL TEXT	MODERN TRANSLATION
Friar Laurence's cell.	Friar Laurence's.
Enter FRIAR JOHN	*Enter FRIAR JOHN*
FRIAR JOHN Holy Franciscan friar! brother, ho!	**FRIAR JOHN** Holy Friar! Hey!
Enter FRIAR LAURENCE	*Enter FRIAR LAURENCE*
FRIAR LAURENCE This same should be the voice of Friar John. Welcome from Mantua: what says Romeo? Or, if his mind be writ, give me his letter.	**FRIAR LAURENCE** This sounds like Friar John. Welcome back from Mantua: what does Romeo say? Or if he wanted to write it down, give me his letter.
FRIAR JOHN Going to find a bare-foot brother out One of our order, to associate me, Here in this city visiting the sick, And finding him, the searchers of the town, Suspecting that we both were in a house Where the infectious pestilence did reign, Seal'd up the doors, and would not let us forth; So that my speed to Mantua there was stay'd.	**FRIAR JOHN** I tried to find someone Another friar to go with me, And this other friar was visiting the sick, When I found him, the police of the town, Thinking everyone in the house Had an infectious disease, Sealed up the house and would not let us out; So I was stuck in Mantua.
FRIAR LAURENCE Who bare my letter, then, to Romeo?	**FRIAR LAURENCE** Who took the letter to Romeo, then?
FRIAR JOHN I could not send it,--here it is again,-- Nor get a messenger to bring it thee, So fearful were they of infection.	**FRIAR JOHN** I could not send it - it's here still And I couldn't get a messenger to go to him, So afraid were they of the infection spreading.
FRIAR LAURENCE Unhappy fortune! by my brotherhood, The letter was not nice but full of charge Of dear import, and the neglecting it May do much danger. Friar John, go hence; Get me an iron crow, and bring it straight Unto my cell.	**FRIAR LAURENCE** What awful luck! I promise The letter was not a nice one but very important, and by not sending it There might be a lot of trouble. Friar John, go now; Get me an iron bar, and bring it right to me.

FRIAR JOHN	**FRIAR JOHN**
Brother, I'll go and bring it thee.	I'll go and get it and bring it to you.
Exit	*Exit*
FRIAR LAURENCE	**FRIAR LAURENCE**
Now must I to the monument alone;	I must go to Juliet's tomb;
Within three hours will fair Juliet wake:	Within a few hours Juliet will wake up:
She will beshrew me much that Romeo	She will be mad that Romeo doesn't know
Hath had no notice of these accidents;	About this whole plan;
But I will write again to Mantua,	But I will write to Romeo again,
And keep her at my cell till Romeo come;	And I will keep Juliet here until Romeo comes;
Poor living corse, closed in a dead man's tomb!	Poor girl, locked up in a dead man's tomb!
Exit	*Exit*

ORIGINAL TEXT	MODERN TRANSLATION
A churchyard; in it a tomb belonging to the Capulets.	A churchyard, in it, a tomb belonging to the Capulet family.
Enter PARIS, and his Page bearing flowers and a torch	*Enter PARIS, and his Page bringing flowers and a torch*
PARIS Give me thy torch, boy: hence, and stand aloof: Yet put it out, for I would not be seen. Under yond yew-trees lay thee all along, Holding thine ear close to the hollow ground; So shall no foot upon the churchyard tread, Being loose, unfirm, with digging up of graves, But thou shalt hear it: whistle then to me, As signal that thou hear'st something approach. Give me those flowers. Do as I bid thee, go.	**PARIS** Give me the torch, and stand away from me: Actually put the torch out, so I am not seen. Wait under those trees over there, Listen out carefully, Non-one shall walk in this churchyard With the loose ground from grave digging, Without you hearing it: If you hear someone then whistle to me, As a signal that you hear someone coming. Give me those flowers and do as I ask.
PAGE [Aside] I am almost afraid to stand alone Here in the churchyard; yet I will adventure.	**PAGE** (quietly) I am scared to wait on my own In this churchyard, but I will do it.
Retires	*Goes away*
PARIS Sweet flower, with flowers thy bridal bed I strew,-- O woe! thy canopy is dust and stones;-- Which with sweet water nightly I will dew, Or, wanting that, with tears distill'd by moans: The obsequies that I for thee will keep Nightly shall be to strew thy grave and weep.	**PARIS** Sweet flower, I will cover your grave with flowers... Where you lay is dust and stones... I will water your flowers with tears Or, if not, with my tears and cries: My habit every night will Be to put flowers on your grave and cry.
The Page whistles	*The Page whistles, signalling that someone is coming*
The boy gives warning something doth approach. What cursed foot wanders this way to-night, To cross my obsequies and true love's rite? What with a torch! muffle me, night, awhile.	My servant is warning me that someone is coming. Who would be wandering around her tonight, To interrupt my grieving and ritual? It's someone with a torch! I will be quiet and hide.
Retires	*Retires*

Enter ROMEO and BALTHASAR, with a torch, mattock, & c	*Enter ROMEO and BALTHASAR, with a torch and axe.*
ROMEO	**ROMEO**
Give me that mattock and the wrenching iron.	Give me that axe and crowbar.
Hold, take this letter; early in the morning	Take this letter; tomorrow morning
See thou deliver it to my lord and father.	Give it to my mum and dad.
Give me the light: upon thy life, I charge thee,	Give me the light, promise
Whate'er thou hear'st or seest, stand all aloof,	Whatever happens next, don't come close,
And do not interrupt me in my course.	Do not interrupt what I am doing.
Why I descend into this bed of death,	The reason I am going into the tomb,
Is partly to behold my lady's face;	Is partly to see Juliet's face;
But chiefly to take thence from her dead finger	But mainly to take a ring from her finger
A precious ring, a ring that I must use	An important ring that I need to use
In dear employment: therefore hence, be gone:	For a good reason: now hurry up and go:
But if thou, jealous, dost return to pry	If you are curious, don't come back to look
In what I further shall intend to do,	At what I am here to do,
By heaven, I will tear thee joint by joint	I promise I will tear you apart
And strew this hungry churchyard with thy limbs:	And put your bodyparts all over the churchyard:
The time and my intents are savage-wild,	This is a wild time and I am feeling wild,
More fierce and more inexorable far	More fierce and impossible to persuade
Than empty tigers or the roaring sea.	than hungry tigers or the wild sea.
BALTHASAR	**BALTHASAR**
I will be gone, sir, and not trouble you.	I will go, and won't bother you.
ROMEO	**ROMEO**
So shalt thou show me friendship. Take thou that:	That will show me how much you care
Live, and be prosperous: and farewell, good fellow.	about me. Take this money,
	live and be rich: and goodbye.
BALTHASAR	**BALTHASAR**
[Aside] For all this same, I'll hide me hereabout:	(quietly) All the same, I'll hide somewhere near:
His looks I fear, and his intents I doubt.	He worries me, and I am sure he lies about what he is here to do.
Retires	*Retires*
ROMEO	**ROMEO**
Thou detestable maw, thou womb of death,	You disgusting mouth of death,
Gorged with the dearest morsel of the earth,	That has eaten the most precious thing on earth,
Thus I enforce thy rotten jaws to open,	I break open your jaws,
And, in despite, I'll cram thee with more food!	And will give you more to eat!
Opens the tomb	*Opens the tomb*

PARIS

This is that banish'd haughty Montague,

That murder'd my love's cousin, with which grief,
It is supposed, the fair creature died;

And here is come to do some villanous shame

To the dead bodies: I will apprehend him.

Comes forward

Stop thy unhallow'd toil, vile Montague!
Can vengeance be pursued further than death?
Condemned villain, I do apprehend thee:
Obey, and go with me; for thou must die.

ROMEO

I must indeed; and therefore came I hither.

Good gentle youth, tempt not a desperate man;

Fly hence, and leave me: think upon these gone;

Let them affright thee. I beseech thee, youth,
Put not another sin upon my head,
By urging me to fury: O, be gone!
By heaven, I love thee better than myself;

For I come hither arm'd against myself:
Stay not, be gone; live, and hereafter say,

A madman's mercy bade thee run away.

PARIS

I do defy thy conjurations,
And apprehend thee for a felon here.

ROMEO

Wilt thou provoke me? then have at thee, boy!

They fight

PAGE

O Lord, they fight! I will go call the watch.

Exit

PARIS

This is Romeo, who is not allowed within
the city,
Who killed Tybalt, which in turn caused
such sadness,
To Juliet that it killed her;
And he has come here to do something
bad
To the dead bodies. I will stop him.

Comes forward

Stop your evil actions, Montague!
Can revenge go further than death?
Villain, I will stop you:
Come with me; you must die.

ROMEO

I must indeed die; and that's why I came
here.
Good man, do not wind me up - I am
desperate
Go away, leave me alone: think about the
dead;
Let them be a warning to you. I beg you,
Don't add another crime to my list,
By making me mad: just go!
I promise, I love you more than I love
myself;
And I've come here to kill myself:
Don't stay, be gone; live and you can later
say,
The sword of a madman made you run
away.

PARIS

I won't do as you ask. I am arresting you as
a criminal.

ROMEO

Will you wind me up to fight? OK, let's
have it!

They fight

PAGE

Oh no, they are fighting! I will go and call
the law.

Exit

PARIS O, I am slain! *Falls* If thou be merciful, Open the tomb, lay me with Juliet. *Dies* **ROMEO** In faith, I will. Let me peruse this face. Mercutio's kinsman, noble County Paris! What said my man, when my betossed soul Did not attend him as we rode? I think He told me Paris should have married Juliet: Said he not so? or did I dream it so? Or am I mad, hearing him talk of Juliet, To think it was so? O, give me thy hand, One writ with me in sour misfortune's book! I'll bury thee in a triumphant grave; A grave? O no! a lantern, slaughter'd youth, For here lies Juliet, and her beauty makes This vault a feasting presence full of light. Death, lie thou there, by a dead man interr'd. *Laying PARIS in the tomb* How oft when men are at the point of death Have they been merry! which their keepers call A lightning before death: O, how may I Call this a lightning? O my love! my wife! Death, that hath suck'd the honey of thy breath, Hath had no power yet upon thy beauty: Thou art not conquer'd; beauty's ensign yet Is crimson in thy lips and in thy cheeks, And death's pale flag is not advanced there. Tybalt, liest thou there in thy bloody sheet? O, what more favour can I do to thee, Than with that hand that cut thy youth in twain To sunder his that was thine enemy? Forgive me, cousin! Ah, dear Juliet, Why art thou yet so fair? shall I believe That unsubstantial death is amorous, And that the lean abhorred monster keeps Thee here in dark to be his paramour? For fear of that, I still will stay with thee; And never from this palace of dim night	**PARIS** Oh, I am dead! *Falls down* Show me mercy And put me in the tomb with Juliet. *Dies* **ROMEO** I promise, I will. Let me look at this face. Mercutio's relative, good Paris! What did my man say, when I was so upset I didn't really listen closely to him? I think He told me Paris was going to marry Juliet: Is that what he said or did I dream it? Or am I mad, hearing him talk of Juliet, To think that was what happened. Oh give me your hand, Like me you've had awful bad luck! I will bury you in an amazing grave; A grave? Oh no! A light, murdered youth, For this is Juliet's tomb, and her beauty makes This vault a place of beauty and light. Dead man lie there, with other dead men. *Laying PARIS in the tomb* How often when men are near death Do they feel happy! Which is called A lightness before death: how can I Call this a lightning? My love, my wife! Death, which has sucked the beauty from you, Has no power over your looks: You are not defeated, but still look pretty Your cheeks and lips are still red, Death has not yet made you pale. Tybalt, is that you in that bloody sheet? What more can I do to help you, Than kill the one who killed you To defeat your enemy? Forgive me cousin! Oh dear Juliet, Why are you still so pretty? Shall I believe that Death is in love, And that monster keeps You here to be his girlfriend? I'm afraid of that, so will stay with you; And never from this place

150

Depart again: here, here will I remain With worms that are thy chamber-maids; O, here Will I set up my everlasting rest, And shake the yoke of inauspicious stars From this world-wearied flesh. Eyes, look your last! Arms, take your last embrace! and, lips, O you The doors of breath, seal with a righteous kiss A dateless bargain to engrossing death! Come, bitter conduct, come, unsavoury guide! Thou desperate pilot, now at once run on The dashing rocks thy sea-sick weary bark! Here's to my love! *Drinks* O true apothecary! Thy drugs are quick. Thus with a kiss I die. *Dies* *Enter, at the other end of the churchyard, FRIAR LAURENCE, with a lantern, crow, and spade* **FRIAR LAURENCE** Saint Francis be my speed! how oft to-night Have my old feet stumbled at graves! Who's there? **BALTHASAR** Here's one, a friend, and one that knows you well. **FRIAR LAURENCE** Bliss be upon you! Tell me, good my friend, What torch is yond, that vainly lends his light To grubs and eyeless skulls? as I discern, It burneth in the Capel's monument. **BALTHASAR** It doth so, holy sir; and there's my master, One that you love. **FRIAR LAURENCE** Who is it?	Leave again: here I will stay With worms that will live in your body; oh here will I stay forever, And forget the bad luck Which has worn me down. Eyes, take your last look! Arms, take your last hug! Lips, oh you, finalise with a kiss The deal you have made to die! Come, bitter conduct, unsavoury guide! Desperate sailor, pushed onto The rocks in your tired ship! Here's to Juliet! *Drinks* Oh honest medicine man! The poison does work fast. So with a kiss I am dead. *Dies* *At the other end of the churchyard, FRIAR LAURENCE, with a light, a crowbar and a spade, enters* **FRIAR LAURENCE** Saint Francis help me to speed up! How often tonight have I tripped over graves? Who is there? **BALTHASAR** I am here, and I am friend that knows you well. **FRIAR LAURENCE** Blessings be on you! Tell me, friend, What light is that over there, which lights up Worms and skulls? It seems to me It is burning in Capulet's tomb. **BALTHASAR** It is, and my boss is in there - someone you care about. **FRIAR LAURENCE** Who is it?

BALTHASAR Romeo.	**BALTHASAR** Romeo.
FRIAR LAURENCE How long hath he been there?	**FRIAR LAURENCE** How long has he been in there?
BALTHASAR Full half an hour.	**BALTHASAR** Half an hour.
FRIAR LAURENCE Go with me to the vault.	**FRIAR LAURENCE** Come with me to the tomb.
BALTHASAR I dare not, sir My master knows not but I am gone hence; And fearfully did menace me with death, If I did stay to look on his intents.	**BALTHASAR** I'd better not, Romeo thinks I am gone; And threatened to kill me, If I stayed to watch what he was doing.
FRIAR LAURENCE Stay, then; I'll go alone. Fear comes upon me: O, much I fear some ill unlucky thing.	**FRIAR LAURENCE** Stay then; I will go on my own. I am afraid: Something bad is happening.
BALTHASAR As I did sleep under this yew-tree here, I dreamt my master and another fought, And that my master slew him.	**BALTHASAR** As I was sleeping under this tree here, I had a dream that Romeo was in a fight, And Romeo killed the person he was fighting with.
FRIAR LAURENCE Romeo!	**FRIAR LAURENCE** Romeo!
Advances	*Advances*
Alack, alack, what blood is this, which stains The stony entrance of this sepulchre? What mean these masterless and gory swords To lie discolour'd by this place of peace?	Oh no! What are these blood stains? They cover the entrance to the tomb. What are these swords doing here Covered in blood in a place of peace?
Enters the tomb	*Enters the tomb*
Romeo! O, pale! Who else? what, Paris too? And steep'd in blood? Ah, what an unkind hour Is guilty of this lamentable chance!	Romeo! Oh he is pale! Who is that? Paris as well? Covered in blood? What a terrible time has taken place here! Juliet is waking up.
The lady stirs.	
JULIET wakes	*JULIET wakes*
JULIET O comfortable friar! where is my lord? I do remember well where I should be,	**JULIET** Oh friar, where is Romeo? I remember where should be,

And there I am. Where is my Romeo?	And I am there. Where is Romeo?
Noise within	*Noise within*
FRIAR LAURENCE	**FRIAR LAURENCE**
I hear some noise. Lady, come from that nest	I hear a noise. Juliet, get up from your bed
Of death, contagion, and unnatural sleep:	Of death, disease and unnatural sleep:
A greater power than we can contradict	A power greater than ours
Hath thwarted our intents. Come, come away.	Has ruined our plans. Let's go.
Thy husband in thy bosom there lies dead;	Romeo is here, lying dead;
And Paris too. Come, I'll dispose of thee	And Paris too. Come on, I'll hide you
Among a sisterhood of holy nuns:	With a sisterhood of nuns:
Stay not to question, for the watch is coming;	Don't stop and ask questions; the law is coming;
Come, go, good Juliet,	Come on Juliet
Noise again	*Noise again*
I dare no longer stay.	I am scared to stay any longer.
JULIET	**JULIET**
Go, get thee hence, for I will not away.	You go away, I am not leaving.
Exit FRIAR LAURENCE	*Exit FRIAR LAURENCE*
What's here? a cup, closed in my true love's hand?	What is this? A cup, held tight in Romeo's hand?
Poison, I see, hath been his timeless end:	Poison, I can see, has killed him:
O churl! drunk all, and left no friendly drop	How rude! He drank it all and left none
To help me after? I will kiss thy lips;	for me? I will kiss your lips Romeo;
Haply some poison yet doth hang on them,	Hopefully some poison will be on them,
To make die with a restorative.	To make me die too.
Kisses him	*Kisses him*
Thy lips are warm.	Your lips are warm.
First Watchman	**First Watchman**
[Within] Lead, boy: which way?	*(within)* Lead the way - where shall we go?
JULIET	**JULIET**
Yea, noise? then I'll be brief. O happy dagger!	Noise? Then I'll be quick. Oh happy knife!
Snatching ROMEO's dagger	*Snatching ROMEO's knife*
This is thy sheath;	My body will sheath you;
Stabs herself	*Stabs herself*
there rust, and let me die.	Rust there and let me die.

Falls on ROMEO's body, and dies	*Falls on ROMEO's body and dies*
Enter Watch, with the Page of PARIS	*Enter Watch, with the Page of PARIS*
PAGE	**PAGE**
This is the place; there, where the torch doth burn.	This is the place; there is the torch burning.
First Watchman	**First Watchman**
The ground is bloody; search about the churchyard:	The ground is covered in blood; look around the churchyard:
Go, some of you, whoe'er you find attach.	Some of you go, arrest anyone you find.
Pitiful sight! here lies the county slain,	What an awful sight! Paris is killed,
And Juliet bleeding, warm, and newly dead,	Juliet bleeding, warm and newly dead,
Who here hath lain these two days buried.	Who has already lied here two days.
Go, tell the prince: run to the Capulets:	Go, tell the prince: run to the Capulets:
Raise up the Montagues: some others search:	Wake up the Montagues: have some others join in the search:
We see the ground whereon these woes do lie;	We see the effect of all this;
But the true ground of all these piteous woes	But to find the cause of all this sadness
We cannot without circumstance descry.	We will need to investigate.
Re-enter some of the Watch, with BALTHASAR	*Re-enter some of the Watch, with BALTHASAR.*
Second Watchman	**Second Watchman**
Here's Romeo's man; we found him in the churchyard.	Here is Romeo's man; we found him in the churchyard.
First Watchman	**First Watchman**
Hold him in safety, till the prince come hither.	Keep a hold on him, the prince will be here in a minute.
Re-enter others of the Watch, with FRIAR LAURENCE	*Re-enter others of the Watch, with FRIAR LAURENCE*
Third Watchman	**Third Watchman**
Here is a friar, that trembles, sighs and weeps:	Here is a friar, that looks very sad and afraid;
We took this mattock and this spade from him,	We took this axe and spade from him,
As he was coming from this churchyard side.	As he was walking along the churchyard.
First Watchman	**First Watchman**
A great suspicion: stay the friar too.	Very suspicious: keep the friar too.
Enter the PRINCE and Attendants	*Enter the PRINCE and Attendants*
PRINCE	**PRINCE**
What misadventure is so early up,	What crime is up so early,
That calls our person from our morning's rest?	That gets us all out of bed?

Original	Modern
Enter CAPULET, LADY CAPULET, and others	*Enter CAPULET, LADY CAPULET, and others*
CAPULET What should it be, that they so shriek abroad?	**CAPULET** What is happening that makes them cry so loud?
LADY CAPULET The people in the street cry Romeo, Some Juliet, and some Paris; and all run, With open outcry toward our monument.	**LADY CAPULET** The people in the street are crying Romeo, Some cry Juliet and some Paris; and all run, Towards this tomb.
PRINCE What fear is this which startles in our ears?	**PRINCE** What terrible thing is everyone shouting about?
First Watchman Sovereign, here lies the County Paris slain; And Romeo dead; and Juliet, dead before, Warm and new kill'd.	**First Watchman** Paris is killed; Romeo dead, Juliet (although already dead), Is alive again and killed.
PRINCE Search, seek, and know how this foul murder comes.	**PRINCE** Investigate how this murder came about.
First Watchman Here is a friar, and slaughter'd Romeo's man; With instruments upon them, fit to open These dead men's tombs.	**First Watchman** Here is a friar, and Romeo's man; They have tools on them, meant to open These tombs of the dead.
CAPULET O heavens! O wife, look how our daughter bleeds! This dagger hath mista'en--for, lo, his house Is empty on the back of Montague,-- And it mis-sheathed in my daughter's bosom!	**CAPULET** Oh no! Wife, look how Juliet is bleeding! The knife's holder is empty on Romeo's back And is stuck in Juliet's chest!
LADY CAPULET O me! this sight of death is as a bell, That warns my old age to a sepulchre.	**LADY CAPULET** Oh, this sight is like a warning bell, That warns my death is coming.
Enter MONTAGUE and others	*Enter MONTAGUE and others*
PRINCE Come, Montague; for thou art early up, To see thy son and heir more early down.	**PRINCE** Montague, you are up early, To see your son and heir.
MONTAGUE Alas, my liege, my wife is dead to-night; Grief of my son's exile hath stopp'd her breath: What further woe conspires against mine age?	**MONTAGUE** My wife died tonight; Sadness over Romeo's exile killed her: What more trouble must I suffer?
Enter CAPULET, LADY CAPULET, and others	*Enter CAPULET, LADY CAPULET, and others*

PRINCE

Look, and thou shalt see.

MONTAGUE

O thou untaught! what manners is in this?
To press before thy father to a grave?

PRINCE

Seal up the mouth of outrage for a while,
Till we can clear these ambiguities,
And know their spring, their head, their
true descent;
And then will I be general of your woes,
And lead you even to death: meantime forbear,
And let mischance be slave to patience.
Bring forth the parties of suspicion.

FRIAR LAURENCE

I am the greatest, able to do least,

Yet most suspected, as the time and place
Doth make against me of this direful murder;
And here I stand, both to impeach and purge
Myself condemned and myself excused.

PRINCE

Then say at once what thou dost know in this.

FRIAR LAURENCE

I will be brief, for my short date of breath

Is not so long as is a tedious tale.
Romeo, there dead, was husband to that Juliet;
And she, there dead, that Romeo's faithful wife:
I married them; and their stol'n marriage-day
Was Tybalt's dooms-day, whose untimely death

Banish'd the new-made bridegroom from the city,
For whom, and not for Tybalt, Juliet pined.
You, to remove that siege of grief from her,

Betroth'd and would have married her perforce
To County Paris: then comes she to me,
And, with wild looks, bid me devise some mean
To rid her from this second marriage,
Or in my cell there would she kill herself.

Then gave I her, so tutor'd by my art,
A sleeping potion; which so took effect
As I intended, for it wrought on her

PRINCE

Look and you will see.

MONTAGUE

Oh Romeo you are so rude!
You are not supposed to die before your
father.

PRINCE

Shut your mouth for a bit,
Until we work out what happened here;
How it started and why it happened;
Then I will be the boss of your sadness,
And may even bring you to death: in the
meantime wait,
Be patient.
Bring forward those we suspect.

FRIAR LAURCNE

I am the greatest, but was able to do
nothing,
I am a suspect because I was here at the
time and place of this awful murder;
And I stand here; you can question me
I've judged and forgiven myself.

PRINCE

Then tell me right away what you know.

FRIAR LAURENCE

I will say it quickly, because I won't be
alive long enough
to tell a boring story.
Romeo, there dead, was married to Juliet;
Juliet, there dead, is Romeo's loving wife:
I married them: and the day they married
Was the day Tybalt died. His badly timed
death
Meant Romeo was not allowed in the city,
For Romeo, and not Tybalt, Juliet cried.
You, her parents, to take her sadness
away,
Engaged her and would have her married
To Paris: then she came to see me,
And asked me to come up with a plan
To get her out of marrying Paris,
Or there and then she would have killed
herself.
I gave her, mixed with my skills,
A sleeping potion, which worked so well
As I planned, that it made her

The form of death: meantime I writ to Romeo,

That he should hither come as this dire night,
To help to take her from her borrow'd grave,
Being the time the potion's force should cease.
But he which bore my letter, Friar John,
Was stay'd by accident, and yesternight
Return'd my letter back. Then all alone
At the prefixed hour of her waking,
Came I to take her from her kindred's vault;
Meaning to keep her closely at my cell,
Till I conveniently could send to Romeo:
But when I came, some minute ere the time
Of her awaking, here untimely lay
The noble Paris and true Romeo dead.
She wakes; and I entreated her come forth,
And bear this work of heaven with patience:

But then a noise did scare me from the tomb;
And she, too desperate, would not go with me,
But, as it seems, did violence on herself.
All this I know; and to the marriage
Her nurse is privy: and, if aught in this
Miscarried by my fault, let my old life
Be sacrificed, some hour before his time,
Unto the rigour of severest law.

PRINCE
We still have known thee for a holy man.
Where's Romeo's man? what can he say in this?

BALTHASAR
I brought my master news of Juliet's death;
And then in post he came from Mantua
To this same place, to this same monument.
This letter he early bid me give his father,
And threatened me with death, going in the vault,
I departed not and left him there.

PRINCE
Give me the letter; I will look on it.
Where is the county's page, that raised the watch?
Sirrah, what made your master in this place?

PAGE
He came with flowers to strew his lady's grave;

And bid me stand aloof, and so I did:
Anon comes one with light to ope the tomb;

Look dead: in the meantime I wrote to Romeo,
To tell him to come here tonight,
To take Juliet from here
When she woke up.
But Friar John, who took my letter,
Was stopped by accident, and last night
Gave me back my letter. Then all alone
At the time she was set to wake up,
I came here to Juliet's tomb;
Meaning to take her back to my place,
Until I could tell Romeo:
But when I got here, just before
Juliet woke, here laid
Paris and Romeo dead.
She woke up, and I begged her to come
with me, and endure this tragic time
with patience:
But a noise scared me away;
And she, too desperate, would not leave,
But, it seems, killed herself.
I know all this, and about the marriage
Her nurse knows: and if any of this
Is my fault, let my life
Be taken,
Under the most severe law.

PRINCE
We know you are a good man.
Where's Romeo's man? Can he add to
this?

BALTHASAR
I told Romeo that Juliet was dead;
And then he came here from Mantua
To this place, to this tomb.
He gave me a letter to give his dad,
And going into the tomb, he threatened to
kill me,
If I didn't go and leave him alone.

PRINCE
Give me the letter; I will look at it.
Where is Paris' page, that called the law?
What made Paris come here?

PAGE
He came with flowers to put on Juliet's
grave;
And told me to leave him alone, so I did:
Someone else came to the tomb;

And by and by my master drew on him;
And then I ran away to call the watch.

PRINCE
This letter doth make good the friar's words,
Their course of love, the tidings of her death:
And here he writes that he did buy a poison
Of a poor 'pothecary, and therewithal
Came to this vault to die, and lie with Juliet.
Where be these enemies? Capulet! Montague!

See, what a scourge is laid upon your hate,
That heaven finds means to kill your joys with love.
And I for winking at your discords too

Have lost a brace of kinsmen: all are punish'd.

CAPULET
O brother Montague, give me thy hand:
This is my daughter's jointure, for no more
Can I demand.

MONTAGUE
But I can give thee more:
For I will raise her statue in pure gold;
That while Verona by that name is known,
There shall no figure at such rate be set
As that of true and faithful Juliet.

CAPULET
As rich shall Romeo's by his lady's lie;

Poor sacrifices of our enmity!

PRINCE
A glooming peace this morning with it brings;
The sun, for sorrow, will not show his head:
Go hence, to have more talk of these sad things;
Some shall be pardon'd, and some punished:
For never was a story of more woe
Than this of Juliet and her Romeo.

Exeunt

And Paris drew his sword out to fight him;
And I ran to the law.

PRINCE
This letter backs up what the friar says,
Their love, him hearing about her death:
And Romeo writes that he bought poison
Off a poor medicine man, and then
Came here to die next to Juliet.
Where are these enemies? Capulet!
Montague!
See what evil results from your hate,
That your joys are killed by love.
And because I didn't take it seriously
enough.
I've lost family too: everyone is punished.

CAPULET
Brother Montague, shake my hand:
This is Juliet's dowry, I can ask no more.

MONTAGUE
I can give you more:
I will make a statue of her in gold;
Whilst this city is known as Verona,
No-one shall praised more highly
Than Juliet.

CAPULET
I will make an equally amazing statue of
Juliet;
They were a poor sacrifice for our rivalry!

PRINCE
A sad peace comes this morning;
The sun is too sad to rise:
Come with me, we will talk more of this:
Some will be let off, others punished:
There was never such a sad story
Than this of Juliet and Romeo.

Exit

Printed in Great Britain
by Amazon